The Pubs of Narberth, Saundersfoot & South-East Pembrokeshire

The Pubs of Narberth, Saundersfoot & South-East Pembrokeshire

by

Keith Johnson

Logaston Press

LOGASTON PRESS
Little Logaston Woonton Almeley
Herefordshire HR3 6QH

First published by Logaston Press 2004
Copyright © Keith Johnson 2004

ISBN 1 904396 21 6

Set in Times New Roman by Logaston Press
and printed in Great Britain by
Bell and Bain Ltd., Glasgow

Contents

Acknowledgments

It may appear that my second book on the history of Pembrokeshire pubs has followed the first one with indecent haste. The reason is simple: I had intended to include Saundersfoot and Narberth in the first book and had completed quite a lot of the research before it became obvious that this would have made the book too unwieldy. Thus part two of my mammoth historical pub crawl of the county was able to follow hard on the heels of the first — but there will now be a chance to sober up for a couple of years before the third volume appears.

As with the first book, this history of the inns of the rural and coastal south-east corner of the county has been cobbled together from a wide variety of sources, some of them more reliable than others. Old newspapers, census returns, travel journals and trade directories have all yielded useful information which has been augmented by the personal memories of many local people, and I am grateful to all those who have so willingly helped me with my researches and pointed me in the direction of a long-forgotten Royal Oak or Masons' Arms.

The area covered by this book is more-or-less the old Narberth Hundred licensing district which comprised the area from Saundersfoot along the coast to Amroth, as far west as Lawrenny and as far north as Robeston Wathen and Llanddewi Velfrey. In order to 'mop up' the rest of the south-east of the county, the villages of Llawhaden, Maenclochog, Rosebush and Llandysilio were added to the brew, whereupon the people of Clunderwen sensibly voted to move from Carmarthenshire into Pembrokeshire which brought another half-dozen pubs into the equation.

When I came to write about the pubs of Pembroke, Pembroke Dock and Tenby, I was fortunate in that several other writers had covered some of the ground before me. In contrast, relatively little has been published about the pubs of the area covered by the present book, although Mr. Roscoe Howells, the Rev. M.G.R. Morris, Mr. Leslie Owen, Mr. A. Eric Evans and Mr. W.R. Morgan have all touched on the subject. As far as unpublished work is concerned, the research material on the pubs of Narberth compiled by Miss Ray Davies and available in Narberth Museum has been an invaluable resource.

I am very grateful to Mr. Roscoe Howells for his encouragement and assistance and for allowing me to quote freely from his work, both published and unpublished. Mr. Howells has also been a great source of illustrations for this book, while I am grateful to all those people who have entrusted me with their old photographs and postcards, in particular Mr. Roger Davies of the Pembroke Collectors Centre and Mr. Gary Davies of Kilgetty.

I owe a particular debt of gratitude to all the staff at the Narberth Museum for their unfailing kindness, help and cups of coffee, and also for the loan of a number of previously unpublished photographs. Thanks also go to Andy Johnson and Ron Shoesmith of Logaston Press for their guidance and patience.

Very many people have provided information for this book and it would be impossible to list every one; my thanks go to them all. In particular I would like to thank the following for their special contributions: Mr. and Mrs. Maurice Cole; Mr. Harry Driver; Mrs. Elizabeth Horne; Mr. G. Hallwood; Mrs. Kay Scourfield; Mr. Owen Vaughan; Mr. John Russell; Mrs. Chris Carvill; Mr. Robert Scourfield; Mr. Michael Whitelock; Mr. Graham Evans; Mr. John Lyons and Mr. Peter Phillips. Also special thanks to the staff of the County Records Office, Haverfordwest; the County Library, Haverfordwest; Tenby Library; Carmarthen Records Office and the National Library of Wales, Aberystwyth.

Thanks are also due to Katy Shoesmith who produced the maps and to Roger Barrett for his help with the index.

And finally my gratitude goes to everyone who bought *The Pubs of Pembroke, Pembroke Dock, Tenby and South Pembrokeshire*, thus ensuring that I would carry on being a Pembrokeshire pub bore for a few more years to come.

Keith Johnson
August 2004

When mighty brown beer was the old Briton's taste,
Our wives they were merry and daughters were chaste,
Their lips were like violets whenever embraced.

'Ere coffee and tea and such slipslops were known,
Our granddames by their fires sat merrily down;
Their bread it was white and their ale it was brown.

When the Spanish Armada on our coasts did bear,
Our sailors took each one a jorum of beer,
Then sent them away with a flea in their ear.

O, the brown beer of Old Britain and old British brown beer!

(The Song of Old British Brown Beer)

CHAPTER ONE

Hotels, Inns & Beer-houses
LEGISLATION & SUNDAY CLOSING

It is sometimes forgotten that Pembrokeshire, and in particular the area covered by this book, once played a major role in the British brewing industry. The baking of partially germinated barley — 'green malt' — in malt kilns was one of the key stages of the traditional brewing process, being crucial to determining the final flavour and colour of the beer. Only the best anthracite was used to fire the kilns of the big brewers like Samuel Allsopp & Sons, Ind Coope and Bass & Co., and for many years this anthracite came from the south Pembrokeshire coalfield.

According to a share prospectus dated 1873, the Bonville's Court collieries were 'well known throughout England' for their 'special quality of coal chiefly used for malting purposes'. Known as 'Myers' Malting Anthracite Coal', this product of the Saundersfoot mines was said to be 'specially suitable for the preparation of best malt'. At nearby Stepaside the collieries were contracted to supply 'malting coal' to the Bass Brewery at Burton upon Trent, while in 1900 it was noted that Bass & Co. were prepared to pay top dollar for Pembrokeshire coal — an extra five shillings per ton over the best Amman Valley anthracite — and that they always took as much as could be spared. It must have been a source of some pride to the colliers of Pembrokeshire that the beer with which they slaked their thirst at night was brewed with the help of the coal which they mined during the day.

Of course, beer and ale, pubs and taverns were in existence long before the days of the big brewery concerns. It is thought that the Romans introduced the concept of the inn to Britain, setting up *tavernæ* along their network of roads where travellers could rest and perhaps enjoy alcoholic refreshment. This was predominantly wine, which the Romans imported from other parts of their empire for the benefit of their legions in Britain, but it is thought that they also brewed a kind of beer from cereals. This idea

1

caught on and by Saxon times there were houses in every village where the men would gather to hold petty courts and to quaff ale out of drinking horns — the real fore-runner of the modern pub.

The earliest ale-houses in Pembrokeshire would probably have been fairly primitive affairs, thatched wooden huts where the inhabitants owned a cauldron capable of boiling up a brew of sweet ale. None of these would have been 'full-time' pubs; they would simply have rustled up a brew when there was a demand, perhaps for a feast day. By the 6th century these ale-houses had become slightly more sophisticated, to the extent of offering a choice of alcoholic beverages. Mead, made from fermented honey, was a well-established favourite of the Celtic people; one early Welsh law specified that a cask of mead should be nine palms high and wide enough to serve as a bathtub for the king and one of his court. And in Wales there were two types of ale — *cwrwf*, which was an everyday kind of ale, and the highly-flavoured (and more expensive) *bragawd* which was spiced up with cinnamon, ginger and cloves.

By AD 745, ale-houses were so widespread, and had gained such a low reputation, that the Archbishop of York had to issue a Canon: 'That no priest go to eat or drink in taverns'. And there were so many inns by the time of King Edgar (959-975) that he tried to limit them to one per village.

The arrival of the Normans in Pembrokeshire and the creation of castle towns such as Pembroke, Tenby, Haverfordwest and Newport led to the establishment of permanent ale-houses in the county. These were often found alongside the market square and close to the church — the historic link between the monasteries and the brewing industry being a strong one. Outside the protection of the towns there were fewer ale-houses — especially in the disputed countryside. These were sometimes known as 'hedge ale-houses' because, with their thatched roof and low walls made out of 'clom' (mud or clay strengthened with straw), they were barely distinguishable from the surrounding vegetation. But as time went by and St. David's began to gain a reputation as a shrine of international importance, so rather more substantial wayside inns were opened to provide hospitality for the pilgrims and later for travelling merchants.

A 14th-century inn.

Moves to regulate the pub trade began at an early date. The Magna Carta included a decree designed to standardise

2

the measurements of wine, ale and corn throughout the land, while in 1266 the Assize of Bread and Ale recognised that these items were the necessities of life and sensibly linked their retail price to the current price of grain. Breaking the assize of ale became an offence which was to keep the manorial courts busy for centuries to come. In 1606, for example, Caria Tanner, a resident of Newport, Pembrokeshire, 'broke the Assize of Ale, selling small measures in illegal measures, therefore she is in mercy 12d'.

The widespread introduction of hops in the 15th century meant that ale slowly began to give way to a new, bitter drink called beer. Despite considerable opposition to this 'pernicious weed' — it was even prohibited for a while — the hop proved very popular with brewers and eventually with drinkers, beer having a sharper flavour and better 'keeping' qualities than the traditional ale. There seems to be no record of large scale hop-growing in Pembrokeshire, although hops were grown in the Carew area at one time (as the name Hop Gardens testifies) and also near Little Haven.

As the number of common ale-houses increased, so did the number of regulations controlling them. It was Henry VII — a son of Pembrokeshire — who introduced Acts in 1495 and 1504 giving local Justices the power to suppress ale-houses which were badly run or which were responsible for keeping men from their all-important archery practice. A further Act in 1553 made a legal distinction between the different kinds of hostelry: ale-houses sold only ale and beer, taverns were restricted to towns and cities and sold only wine (though later they sold beer as well), while inns also offered accommodation. Most of these places would have brewed their own beer, although in the smaller houses, where the part-time ale-house

A 14th-century tavern with a cellar in which to keep the wine.

3

keeper had a trade which occupied most of his day, it was the practice to buy beer from better-equipped inns and later from full-time brewers.

Although both Tenby and Haverfordwest were notable wine-importing centres at one time, it seems unlikely that there were too many taverns in Pembrokeshire that offered only wine — ale and beer were the order of the day for the Welsh lower classes. However a complaint to the Star Chamber in 1602 stated that an Irish priest who visited Pembroke was 'a comon haunter of alhouses and wintaverns', so there must have been wine bars in the town 400 years ago. Even so, most of the wine that the merchants shipped into the county was destined for the castles and manor houses of the gentry; according to the bards who sang his praises, Tomas ap Phylip of Picton Castle once took delivery of a shipment of 20 tuns of wine — about 5,000 gallons.

Despite this impressive statistic, the Elizabethan historian George Owen thought that heavy drinking was rare in Pembrokeshire. However he did concede that an influx of Irish settlers into the county in the days of Henry VIII had given the locals a taste for whiskey. As Owen explained:

> Those Irish people here do use their country trade in making of Aqua Vitae in great abundance which they carry to be sold abroad the country on horseback and otherwise, so that weekly you may be sure to have Aqua Vitae to be sold at your door, and by means thereof it is grown to be an usual drink in most men's houses instead of wine.

By the beginning of the 17th century, there were plenty of licensed ale-houses in Pembrokeshire — and more than a few unlicensed ones as well. In 1606, the Court Leet and View of Frankpledge in Newport dealt with the case of a tailor named Richard ap Ievan and ten others who 'kept taverns in their houses and sold ale without licence'. And in 1615, Hugh Johnes of Llanychaer and Thomas Price of St. Dogmael's were separately presented at the Great Sessions for 'keeping without a licence a common tippling house and for selling ale and beer'. What was unusual about this case is that as well as running an illicit shebeen, Price was better known as the Rev. Thomas Price, vicar of St. Dogmael's!

In the towns, the inns and ale-houses tended to cluster around market squares and harbours where there was always a lively trade. Quay Street in Haverfordwest and the area around Tenby Quay would have had their share of rough and ready 'sailortown' pot-houses, while the pubs on Fishguard Square, Narberth Square and the East End of Pembroke came alive on market days and fair days. Out in the countryside, wherever there was hard work to be done, ale-houses — legal and otherwise — sprang up to provide refreshment for the labouring man. Bread, cheese and 'table beer' —

4

as opposed to strong ale — sustained the quarryman and labourer, ploughman and collier throughout the long working day.

Many of the smaller country ale-houses had names designed to encourage the passer-by to enter — some of which live on in the name of Pembrokeshire localities. There were several ale-houses called 'Step Inn', as well as a 'Venture Inn' (now Venterin) near Lampeter Velfrey, the 'Stop-and-Call' at Goodwick and the 'Step Aside' near Kilgetty. It is also likely that Cold Inn near East Williamston was once 'Call Inn' — a rather more inviting name. With the Cleddau River carving its way through the heart of the county there were numerous ferry crossings, and all of these had an ale-house on at least one side of the river — usually run by the ferry-man and his wife.

In the towns, inns of a more substantial nature had been established, perhaps following the dissolution of the monasteries when pilgrims could no longer seek shelter in abbeys and other religious houses. The sadly-demolished Swan in Haverfordwest was said to date from the 16th century, while there are references to both the King's Arms in Pembroke and to the King's Arms in Tenby in 1617. These inns offered reasonable accommodation for travellers, stabling for their horses, and a ready meal, but the golden age of the inn — the era of the stage-coach — had yet to arrive and they were far from the bustling establishments they were to become.

The 18th century saw a further development with the arrival of purpose-built public houses. Where ale-houses were basically cottages with a room in which refreshments could be enjoyed, the public houses might have several rooms to cater for the different classes of drinker (but without offering the accommodation which would have turned them into inns). This competition had the effect of dragging many ale-houses 'up-market', although this increased respectability didn't prevent the criminal classes — the pick-pockets, prostitutes, smugglers and highway robbers — from continuing to frequent the seedier houses at the bottom end of the scale.

Another change in the 18th century was in the amount of spirits being consumed, particularly cheap brandy and gin. While duty had to be paid on beer, spirits remained exempt for a good many years, so that the consumption of spirits increased from about half a million gallons in 1684 to eight million gallons in 1743 — an increase of well over a gallon per person per year. It took a succession of 'Gin Acts' to curb the dram shops and gin palaces and persuade people to turn back to the relatively healthy consumption of beer, ale and — increasingly — porter.

This latter drink was a specially blended mild beer which took its name from its popularity among London's market porters, and porter breweries soon sprang up all over the country — notably that of Samuel Whitbread in Chiswell Street in the City of London. This also led to another new development — the brewer's dray. Where once the ale-house keeper would have been expected to fetch the casks from the brewery himself, now the brewer made regular deliveries to all the pubs on his patch — a practice which eventually led to the 'tied house'. Although brewery-to-pub delivery was initially confined to the larger centres of population, horse-drawn brewer's drays inevitably found their way onto the streets and country lanes of Pembrokeshire.

Up to this time, and for many years to come, the easiest way to travel to Pembrokeshire was by sea, and little in the way of coaching inns had developed in the county. This changed in the late 18th century with the establishment of a packet service to Ireland from Hakin Point and also the emergence of Tenby as a fashionable sea-bathing resort. The coach road to Hakin Point ran by way of St. Clears, Llanddowror, Tavernspite, Narberth and Haverfordwest and several coaching inns were established as posting stages along this route, including the Picton at Llanddowror, the Plume of Feathers at Tavernspite, the Golden Lion in Narberth, the Coach and Horses in Robeston Wathen and the Castle in Haverfordwest. On the road which branched south to Pembroke, there were the Milford Arms in Saundersfoot, the White Lion in Tenby and the Golden Lion and Green Dragon in Pembroke itself. These were all substantial buildings with good rooms and plenty of stabling, and as often as not had been built at the instigation of the local squire.

A horse-drawn dray delivers casks for local wine and spirit merchant
James Williams in Church Street, Narberth, in the 1930s.

Picture courtesy of the Wilson Museum, Narberth

Many coaching inns were well-run establishments; some weren't. According to John Byng, writing in the 18th century:

> The innkeepers are insolent, the hostlers are sulky, the chambermaids are pert and the waiters are impertinent; the meat is tough, the wine is foul, the beer is hard, the sheets are wet, the linen is dirty and the knives are never clean'd!

It is to be hoped that Pembrokeshire's inns were run to a better standard, though most late-18th-century travellers settled for describing them as 'middling' or 'tolerable' at best.

While the number of larger, well-appointed inns and public houses continued to increase, approved and licensed by the magistrates, there were still large numbers of smaller and humbler houses which operated in the grey area between ale-house and unlicensed 'shebeen'. In 1779, several people in Steynton, Pill and Hubberston were convicted of 'selling ale and strong beer without being licensed so to do', and as time went by it became apparent that gin drinking was once again on the increase and that the dodgier ale-houses were turning into dram-shops.

Various Acts were passed in the 1820s in an attempt to reverse this trend, culminating in the 1830 Beer Act. This was designed to encourage the consumption of beer at the expense of spirits — a move which would boost the country's agriculture and brewing industries and also improve health. Beer was widely considered to be a wholesome and health-giving drink, much more so than water which was often of a dubious quality — especially in the towns. For example, when Milford Sunday School held a New Year's Day treat in 1818, nearly 200 children enjoyed a meal of roast beef and plum pudding 'and afterwards ale supplied by Mr. G. Starbuck and Mr. R. Byers' — Byers being the local surgeon.

The 1830 Beer Act duly abolished all duty on beer and brought into being the 'beer-shop' or 'beer-house'. For the cost of two guineas, any householder could obtain a beer-house licence which would permit the sale of beer and cider only — as opposed to the fully licensed public houses which could also sell wine and spirits. The result of this new legislation can be easily imagined — beer-houses by the thousand opened up all over the country. Former 'shebeens' entered the fold of legitimacy, while masons and blacksmiths, farmers, coopers and carpenters took the opportunity to sell beer as a sideline to their regular trade. Within a year of the Act coming into force there were 24,000 new beer-houses in Britain and the figure had reached 46,000 by 1836. In the twin towns of Pembroke and Pembroke Dock there were 45 beer-houses in 1840 while Milford Haven had 24. 'Everybody is drunk', reported Sydney Smith soon after the Beer Act came into force. 'Those who are not singing are sprawling'.

These new drinking premises were often called 'Tom and Jerry shops' after a pair of dissolute characters in Pierce Egan's serialised novel *Life in London*, or sometimes 'Kiddleywinks'. They were often badly run, and as the Haverfordwest weekly newspaper *Potter's Electric News* noted: 'Beer-shop owners prey upon labouring men who earn their money like horses — and then spend it like asses'. They also attracted a seedy clientele. 'The beer-shop keeper collects about him the very dregs of society. It is in these places that robberies are planned and crimes committed. The beer-shop keeper is too frequently the banker of the thief'.

Because of their very nature, beer-houses are difficult to research. The Beer Act made no provision for the keeping of records of licences, and numerous 'Kiddleywinks' came and went without leaving any trace other than a vague folk memory. Several of these were *ad hoc* affairs which opened to take advantage of such things as the arrival of gangs of navvies to build a road or railway and which closed again following their departure. Others lasted much longer, and there was hardly a street in Pembroke Dock which didn't have a beer-house or three to cater for the town's hard-drinking population of shipwrights, seamen and soldiers.

Running parallel with the spread of the beer-shop came the rise of Nonconformity and also the growing influence of the temperance movement. This movement had become organised as far back as 1828, and — ironically perhaps — had strongly supported the Beer Act and its aim of getting people to stop drinking gin. Its members pledged themselves to abstain from all spirits — except for medicinal purposes — and only to drink beer and wine 'in moderation'. This wasn't enough for some of the hard-line reformers who went even further and advocated total abstinence. These teetotallers, who often clashed with their more 'wishy-washy' temperance colleagues, embarked on a high-profile campaign aimed at persuading people to give up the demon drink altogether. Meetings were held up and down the country at which reformed drunkards in their Sunday best were paraded in front of the audience as living examples of the benefits of total abstinence.

One such character who addressed a meeting in Ebenezer Chapel, Haverfordwest in January 1839 was introduced as 'a reformed drunkard from Milford'. He gave what was described in the *Welshman* newspaper as 'an exciting, though melancholic' account of himself, explaining that for 17 years he had 'served the monster intemperance'. During this time he had been notorious for his habitual drunkenness, but he had signed the pledge 12 months before and was now 'in every respect more happy than when he was in the habit of indulging in the intoxicating draught'.

In Narberth, a Total Abstinence Society was formed in 1837 and in 1841 the *Welshman* reported that there were 'numerous' total abstainers in the town

Haverfordwest Temperance Council.

Sat., April 4, to Thurs., April 9.

Christian Temperance

Campaign

Will be conducted by MR.

JAS. GILLESPIE

Musical Missioner and Temperance Advocate.

Composer and Hymn Writer, Editor of "Mission Melodies"

Saturday, April 4th, at 7.30 Temperance Hall—Great Temperance Demonstration & Welcome Meeting

Sunday, April 5th, Three Great Meetings in the

TEMPERANCE HALL.

3 p.m. Subject, "Wanted a Man." Open to all.
6 p.m. Special Meeting for Boys and Girls.
8 p.m. Great United Meeting. Subject, "Drink the Destroyer."

Monday, April 6th. at 7.30. **Albany Chapel.**
Subject— **' EXCUSES EXAMINED'**

Tuesday, April 7th, at 7.30. **Hill Park Chapel**
Subject— **'THE CRY OF THE CHILDREN'**

Wednesday, April 8th, 7.30. **Bethesda Chapel**
Subject— **'THE POWER OF DRINK.'**

Thurs , Ap.9th, 7.30. **Wesleyan Schoolroom**
Farewell Lecture and Musical Recital, entitled
'LOVE COURTSHIP & MARRIAGE.'
Admission on this special night by Ticket 6d. each.

Mr. GILLESPIE will sing at every Meeting.
The Singing begins earlier than advertised time of Meeting.
Come and hear the Soul-stirring Solos and Choruses.

A WELCOME FOR YOU

Admission Free *Questions Invited*
Ask at Hall Door for a copy of " GOOD WORDS."

A week of activities on behalf of the Haverfordwest Temperance Council, led by the 'musical missionary' James Gillespie.

of Pembroke whose battle-cry was: 'Honour to the Welsh water-drinkers! Destruction to the publicans and sinners of Cymru!' To begin with they were fighting a losing battle. The number of pubs and beer-houses continued to grow, and although the coaching inns were badly hit by the arrival of the railways, this was more than offset by the number of pubs created to serve the new form of transport, with Railway Inns and Railway Taverns being opened in every town and nearly every village on the line — from Johnston and Wiston to Jameston, Lamphey and Penally. Quarrying villages such as West Williamston, Ludchurch and Cilgerran were awash with pubs and beer-houses and it was said that every house in Hakin that wasn't a licensed pub was an unlicensed one.

Gradually, however, the tide began to turn. The Lord's Day Observance Society had been founded in the same year as the British and Foreign Temperance Society, and the two movements soon found plenty of common ground on which to campaign. They achieved some early success with the passing of the Lord's Day Act of 1848 which prevented pubs from opening before 1pm on a Sunday.

Attempts to restrict Sunday opening still further in 1855 led to street riots in London; even so an Act was passed soon afterwards restricting Sunday opening to the hours of 1pm to 3pm and 5pm to 11pm. In Pembrokeshire, as in the rest of Wales, the campaign against Sunday drinking was spearheaded by the Nonconformists. Each wave of religious revival which swept across Wales was accompanied by a wave of temperance activity — in Cilgerran it was claimed that the thunder of one revival had turned the beer sour.

In 1860 came the first movement towards 'early closing' — a laudable scheme designed to give shop-workers in the towns a mid-week half-day holiday. Sports clubs — most famously Sheffield Wednesday — were formed in many places to provide 'healthful and innocent amusement' for young men with time to kill. Cricket clubs were formed all over Pembrokeshire; as one of the founders of the Pembroke club pointed out:

> If these young men are not on the cricket field, there will probably, many of them at least, be found in the pursuit of some vice or sensual pleasure — perhaps guzzling like brute-beasts in the pot-houses with which the town of Pembroke unfortunately abounds.

By the end of the 1860s there was a growing consensus that the beer-house had long outlived its usefulness and that the number of pubs in the country needed to be curtailed. The 1869 Wine and Beer-house Act brought all licensed premises under the control of the magistrates. This effectively meant that no new beer-houses were opened while many of the existing ones closed down, their trade not being sufficient to warrant the cost and effort of applying for a justices' licence. The Aberdare Act of 1872 added to the burden of legislation on the drinking trade, curtailing drinking hours, increasing fines for licensing offences, prohibiting the sale of liquor to under-16s and generally making life difficult for the landlord. (This Act was so unpopular that it was blamed for the fall of Gladstone's government two years later; Disraeli's administration increased the opening hours by 30 minutes as a mark of appreciation).

In Wales, Sunday opening remained the biggest bugbear of the temperance brigade. In Calvinist Scotland the pubs had been closed on the Sabbath since 1853, and when Ireland introduced Sunday closing in 1878, the Welsh campaigners were determined to be next. Temperance and chapel leaders claimed (with some justification) that the majority of people in Wales were behind them — although a public meeting held in Tenby in February 1880 to press for Sunday closing was 'miserably attended'. In the industrialised areas of Wales, the sabbatarians received powerful support from the iron-masters and the coal-owners who were fed up with half their workforce turning up for the Monday morning shift still drunk from the excesses of the previous day.

Wales was ripe for Sunday closing, and when a private member's Bill, introduced by Flint MP John Roberts, received its third reading in August 1881, the Welsh Sunday Closing Act duly entered the statute books.

In Pembrokeshire, many of the big landowners were also active supporters of temperance — among their tenants, if not on a personal level! As a result, estates like Stackpole, Lamphey and Lawrenny were without a public house for many years — to the great benefit of pubs in villages like Maidenwells, Hundleton and Landshipping which were just over the border in neighbouring estates.

Towards the end of the 19th century and in the first part of the 20th century, efforts continued to be made to reduce the numbers of public houses and also to standardise their lay-out. Magistrates found themselves with the power to take away licences for petty offences or because the lay-out of a pub did not meet their approval. And since many of the magistrates were chapel deacons and temperance-supporting landowners themselves, they did not hesitate to use this power — even if it meant a family's loss of livelihood. Even this consideration was met by an Act of 1904 which established the principle of compensation for publicans whose licence had been suppressed through no fault of their own (although in practice most of the compensation went to the owner of the property, rather than the publican who was usually a tenant).

The first pub in Pembrokeshire to be axed under the compensation scheme was the St Dogmells in Hakin, and the Act was eventually responsible for the closure of nearly 100 pubs in the county, among them noted houses like the Albion on Tenby Harbour, the Tower Inn in St. David's, the Gun Tavern in Pembroke Dock and the Sailors' Arms in Lower Fishguard. However, the publicans did not go down without a fight. Pembroke Dock Licensed Victuallers Association was formed in 1909 'for combination to combat the forces acting against them' and the Pembrokeshire LVA followed a year later with about 50 members. One of their aims

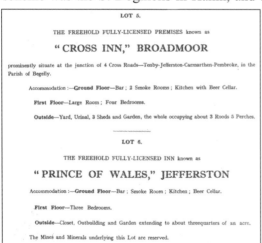

Two village pubs on the Pembrokeshire coalfield came under the hammer in the early 1930s — but not the rights to the minerals lying below.

was to obtain an 'impartial bench of magistrates' to adjudicate on the renewal of licences. All too often the magistrates would instruct the police to object to a certain licence, and then rule on the objection themselves — a 'disgraceful' situation according to Mr. S. McCulloch, the first president of the Pembrokeshire LVA.

The interior of the Cresselly Arms at Cresswell Quay hasn't changed much since this photograph was taken in 1914. On the left is landlord Jim Davies — 'Jim the Pub'.

Picture courtesy of the Cresselly Arms.

However, it has to be said that the magistrates often had statistics on their side. In the 1890s Narberth boasted 23 pubs for a resident population of just 1,200. And in 1912 there were 81 on licences and three off licences granted for Pembroke Borough, giving an average of one licensed house for every 190 residents compared with the national average of one for every 400. Thus Pembroke Borough had twice as many pubs per head of population as the rest of Britain in 1912.

The Defence of the Realm Act also took a toll on Pembrokeshire pubs following the outbreak of the First World War. The Act meant the introduction of even tighter licensing laws aimed at preventing drunkenness among servicemen, dockers, munitions workers and the like. In Lloyd George's opinion: 'Drink is doing us more damage in the war than all the German submarines put together' — but as someone who had once pressed for total prohibition in Wales, he might not have been entirely objective. Opening hours were curtailed, while one of the daftest rules brought in by the Act was the 'no treating' law. Under this rule no-one was allowed to buy a round of drinks or even buy his mate a pint; this was thought to encourage excessive drinking. In 1916 James Gray, landlord of the eminently respectable Avondale in Hakin, was fined ten shillings for allowing 'treating' in the pub.

He was lucky not to lose his licence. With a mass of new rules and regulations to fall foul of, it was inevitable that many landlords found themselves in court. And when they appeared before the bench there would be the inevitable clamour from the temperance brigade for the pubs to be shut.

Three noted Pembrokeshire landlords from the 1950s are in the front row of this photograph. Left to right: Wiffie Vaulk of the Bush in Tenby, Jim Davies of the Cresselly Arms (where the picture was taken) and Tommy Nicholas of the Dragon in Narberth.

Picture courtesy of Mr. Maurice Cole.

Many were, and when the troops returned from the trenches it was often to find that their favourite local had been forced to close. Wartime 'casualties' in Pembroke Dock alone included the Foresters' Arms, the Albert, the Sun and the Duke of York.

Licensing restrictions were gradually lifted following the end of the war — although Sunday closing remained sacrosanct. The number of pubs continued to fall, both as a result of the still-active redundancy committee and the economic depression, while changing social habits (and weaker beer) meant the number of drunks on the street fell dramatically. In 1908, 99 people had been convicted of drunkenness in Pembroke Borough; by the 1930s the figure was down to half a dozen each year.

As attitudes changed, and people began to look upon the village pub as a convivial social centre rather than a den of iniquity, so support for the temperance movement began to wane. By the time the Second World War came, the tide had turned to the extent that calls for a return to the licensing restrictions of 1914 were dismissed out of hand. In his excellent history of brewing in Wales, *Prince of Ales*, Brian Glover quotes Quintin Hogg (later Lord Hailsham) as stating in 1939:

> The Temperance Council must clearly understand that the national emergency is not a moment to introduce temperance propaganda under the cloak of national necessity. Beer is the innocent pleasure of many millions, especially those who bear the brunt today.

Such a sentiment — a million miles from that of Lloyd George 25 years earlier — shows how much attitudes had changed. The temperance movement was in retreat, although the redundancy committee continued to pick off pubs well into the 1950s — the Crown and Anchor and the Bell and Lion in Pembroke Dock were both closed in 1953.

*The results of a typical Pembrokeshire pub makeover in the 1960s/'70s.
This is the Drovers' Arms at Puncheston.*

With the post-war growth of tourism, inns began to be seen as an amenity and Sunday closing in Wales became increasingly regarded as an anachronism and a hindrance to the industry. A new Licensing Act in 1961 paved the way for each county to decide by a referendum (held every seven years) if it wanted Sunday drinking. The three west Wales counties of Pembrokeshire, Carmarthenshire and Cardiganshire voted to stay 'dry' in 1961, but in November 1968, alone of the three, Pembrokeshire voted to become 'wet'.

The 1960s and early '70s also saw the opening of a number of new pubs in the tourist areas of the county — the Snooty Fox, the Lawrenny Arms, the Dial Inn and the Miracle Inn among others — and the enlargement and refurbishment of many more. Sadly, this refurbishment was often at the cost of the character of the old inn, and a pub guide of the time called *The Inn Crowd* shows (unintentionally) the widespread damage that was caused by the over-enthusiastic introduction of formica, leatherette, exposed stonework and fake beams covered with equally fake horse-brasses.

Fortunately a good number of old Pembrokeshire pubs managed to avoid this kind of makeover, so that the county still has a wide range of unspoilt taverns — from 'Bessie's' in the Gwaun Valley to the Charlton in Pembroke Dock and the Old Point House in Angle. And although well-established pubs continue to close — the Coach and Horses in Narberth, the Railway Inn in Pembroke and the Sir Charles Whetham in Milford Haven are all recent victims — a glance at the pages of this book will show that this is simply part of an on-going process that has seen pubs come and go throughout the centuries as taste and circumstances changed with the passing years.

CHAPTER TWO

New Hedges to Begelly

The first book in this series on Pembrokeshire pubs ended at the **Three Bells** just outside Tenby. The 'pub-crawl' continues half a mile or so to the north, where a young widow named Ann Bowen ran a cottage ale-house in the early 1840s. This was close to the tollgate between Tenby and New Hedges, and although its name isn't recorded, a newspaper report of 1843 referred to the **Royal Oak** 'near Tenby', which may be the same place.

In the village of New Hedges, the Lawrence family has been involved in running pubs for a century and a half. Farmer John Lawrence ran the **Green Dragon** from 1841 to 1859 followed by his wife Margaret in 1861. Their son Benjamin Lawrence had taken over by 1865, but he seems to have concentrated on the farming aspect and the ale-house closed in about 1870. The Green Dragon was part of the 18th-century farmstead known as Rumbleyway House and was located in the wing of the building which fronted the road; rings in the wall have been found where customers would have tethered their horses.

The village was without a pub for the best part of a century until the **Hunters Moon** was opened in the early 1960s with Mr. W.G. Lawrence as proprietor. Built on the site of an old byre and barn alongside Rumbleyway House, the Hunters Moon was remarkable in that it incorporated massive oak beams and oak flooring from Earl Cawdor's former mansion at Stackpole Court which was being demolished at the time. Bookcases from the mansion also found their way into the new pub, while the Cawdor family's horse-drawn hearse was converted into a bar counter! According to a guide book written in about 1970 'Another interesting feature about this wayside inn is that it was built by one stonemason and one carpenter, together with members of the owner's family. It was designed entirely by the proprietress, Mrs. R.C. Lawrence'.

It was Mrs. Lawrence — a keen horsewoman and rider to hounds — who gave the pub its unusual name and filled it with a fascinating collection of

The unusual interior of the Hunters Moon, complete with beams and furniture salvaged from Stackpole Court.
Picture courtesy of Mrs. R.C. Lawrence.

The Hunters Moon has become the New Hedges Tavern.

antiques and memorabilia. The Lawrences ran the Hunters Moon until 1979, since when it has changed hands a couple of times and has been unimaginatively rechristened the **New Hedges Tavern**.

For about 20 years the **Snooty Fox** was a popular country pub on the Devonshire Drive. Created out of two adjoining cottages in the early 1970s, it was run initially as a café by Mr. Leslie Duncan before being converted into a pub. It was subsequently run for a few years by Mr. Colin Ray while Mr. Dennis Brace was the landlord from 1984 to 1994 in which year the building reverted to being two cottages.

The **Masons' Arms** was at Moreton, in the heart of the Pembrokeshire coalfield. William Davies (who was a master mason) opened this pub and ran it between 1864 and 1875, the business bringing in a tidy £50 a year from the thirsty colliery workers. He was then given notice to quit by new landlords, the Saundersfoot & Tenby Collieries Co. Ltd., who said they wanted the property as housing for the foreman of Moreton Colliery. Davies reluctantly moved out and built himself a new pub — the Commercial — on land near Saundersfoot station. However the Masons' Arms then carried on as a pub for a couple more years, the licence being held by George Blizzard — who just happened to be one of the main shareholders in the Saundersfoot & Tenby Collieries Co. Ltd. But by the end of the decade the colliery company had been forced into liquidation and the Masons' Arms had closed for good.

Just off the main road, on the Clayford Lane to East Williamston, was the **Pear Tree**. This was the cottage home of the Ollin family long before it became a pub, the name being shared with the nearby Pear Tree coal-pit. The licensee for many years was Stephen Ollin, a disabled collier who had probably opened his house as a pub when he was no longer able to work in the mines. He evidently kept long hours. 'Many complaints are made by women whose husbands are kept at this house all night, and if that continues the licence will be refused next year', the magistrates warned Mr. Ollin in 1872, at the same time as they fined him 20 shillings for serving beer out of hours on Good Friday. The warning must have been heeded, as the Ollins continued to run the Pear Tree for many years afterwards. In fact, when Stephen Ollin died in 1887 the licence passed to his widow Mary and she was there until her death in 1898. Alfred Badham then took over temporarily but failed to persuade the magistrates to allow him a full transfer of the licence and the pub duly closed. A new private house — still called Pear Tree — was built on the site some 20 years ago.

The village of Wooden may have had a pub in the distant past. The **New Inn** was run by Mary Gunter from 1812 to 1823 and thereafter by her husband, colliery agent Joseph Brinn. Where it was located isn't known, but since the couple were living in Wooden at the time of the 1841 census it may be that the pub was in the village. More recently the **Woodridge** has opened in Wooden as a popular family pub and leisure complex.

In Pentlepoir is the **Fountain Head** which was kept by William Allen from 1822 to 1827 and which seems to have taken its name from the many freshwater springs which rise in the vicinity. The 1841 census shows 'Persilla' (Priscilla) Allen, aged 40 at the Fountain Head and among her employees was a 26-year-old farm servant, William Thomas. By the time of the 1851 census they were man and wife, and William Thomas held the licence until about 1870 and farmed 18 acres. Isaac Cadwallader took up the tenancy of the pub at Michaelmas 1871 but soon handed on to Daniel Davies who remained for three years before moving to run the Brewery Tap in Saundersfoot. David Thomas took over and was still there in 1880. Thomas Williams was the landlord from 1891 to 1900 followed by various licensees including Lionel Brook from the nearby Commercial, Mrs. Margaret Jenkins and Benjamin Waters who was there from 1912 to 1916.

Jack Evans, who was the long-serving landlord from 1917 until the early 1950s, is remembered as running a very tight ship — 'any trouble and you were out of the door'. It was a James Williams house at the time and Mr. Evans and his wife Beatrice also farmed the smallholding which was attached to the pub. Following the Evans' retirement, their son Mr. Wyndham Evans — a Tenby motor dealer — purchased the pub from the brewery. He

The Fountain Head still looked like a farmhouse in the 1960s.

Picture courtesy of the *Western Telegraph.*

A more recent view of the Fountain Head.

sold it to Dennis Morgan of Yerbeston Gate who was in charge for much of the 1960s while Eric Caine moved there from the Hean Castle in Saundersfoot in about 1970.

The Fountain Head was altered and extended in the 1960s and '70s to take advantage of its position on the tourist route into Tenby and Saundersfoot, with much of the farmland being turned into a caravan site. Recent licensees have included local builder Ralph Harries, Ken French and Andrew Williams.

The **Evening Star** almost opposite was another farm-cum-ale-house where carters and coachmen would stop for a pint and a chat while resting the horses after the long pull up from Begelly. Thomas Lewis was there from the 1840s to the 1860s and he also farmed 30 acres. An inquest was held at the Evening Star in 1867 into the accidental death of a young miner at Bonville's Court colliery. Thomas Lewis' daughter, Mary, and her husband, James Thomas, kept the pub from 1871 to 1899, after which their son, Thomas Lewis Thomas carried on the family tradition until 1917. In that year the Evening Star was deemed surplus to requirements by the local magistrates who refused to renew the licence and paid out a derisory £10 in compensation to the publican.

The **Commercial** was situated near Saundersfoot station, just above the railway bridge. Publican and master mason William Davies built the Commercial in 1875 after he had been forced to close the Masons' Arms in

Moreton. The new pub cost him £250, only for Narberth magistrates initially to refuse him permission to transfer the licence from the Masons' to the new premises. Mr. Davies doggedly reapplied, producing a petition 'numerously and influentially signed' claiming that the new pub would be 'a great boon to the public frequenting the watering place of Saundersfoot'. Grudgingly, and despite fierce opposition from the proprietors of the nearby Evening Star, the magistrates eventually approved the switch of licence.

William, his wife Sarah, and their six children remained at the Commercial until 1895. Lionel Brook was the 'cheery' licensee from 1896 to 1903, while Walter Williams was there from 1907 through to the 1940s. The pub, known locally as 'The Dobbin', was built on a bank and was reached via a flight of nine steps. It was described in 1911 as having a smoking room, two other public rooms, kitchen, living room and cellar, with three front bedrooms upstairs and a coach house and stable to the rear. At this time it was thriving on the trade generated by the local collieries and by the proximity of the station.

By 1947, however, the pub was in a sorry state. The collieries were closed, Walter Williams had died and the 'Dobbin' was being run by his widow Marjorie who was almost completely blind. The building had no electricity, and water had to be fetched from a stand-pipe 250 yards away. There was an earth lavatory at the back, but the old urinal had fallen down. The wooden floor of the bar was rotten to the extent that it had two large holes in it, and a policeman who inspected the premises noted: 'The bar, cellar, kitchen, stairs and landing are in a deplorable state, the walls requiring replastering and the woodwork in need of extensive repair'. Not surprisingly the Commercial was closed shortly afterwards on health grounds and after standing empty for some years it was eventually pulled down.

The parish of Begelly was once an important coal-mining area, with rich anthracite seams below the ground and a surface scarred with spoil heaps and mine workings. Records show that Begelly Colliery was in full production by the 1770s and there were numerous other mines in the area of Thomas Chapel, Broom and Hackett. The main route from Tenby to Narberth passed through Begelly village, and when the new turnpike road from St. Clears to Hobbs Point was built in the 1830s it crossed the old north-south road at what became known as Begelly Cross. The commercial potential of this crossroads site was obvious, and an advertisement duly appeared in the *Welshman* newspaper for February 1834 offering a plot of land at Begelly 'contiguous to the New Line of Road from St. Clears to Pembroke Dock and Hobbs Point, well situated for the erection of an Inn and Posting House'. It came with 50 acres of arable land and appears to have been the plot on which the **Begelly Arms** was built. Certainly the pub was up and running by 1838, boasting a dining parlour, drawing room, breakfast parlour and bar, six bedrooms, an excellent kitchen (flagged), brewing

A view of the Begelly Arms in the days of Alfred Davies,
cabinet-maker, undertaker and occasional dentist.

kitchen, dairy, cellars, four-stall stable and coach-house, garden, piggery and
hen-house. 'The house is situated on a very great thoroughfare for travelling',
stated a notice in the *Carmarthen Journal*. 'The London Mail goes by it every
morning to Hobbs Point and returns the same night'.

Elizabeth Evans was the licensee in 1841, the licence passing on
marriage to her husband Thomas Lewis a few years later. The inn was a
convenient place to hold inquests on workers killed in the collieries — some
of them as young as 12 years; it was also used as an occasional courtroom by
the local justices. However, it was at Narberth court that landlord Lewis
appeared in August 1853, charged with threatening to kill his wife Elizabeth.
He was bound over to keep the peace for 12 months, but just three months
later Lewis again assaulted his wife and was jailed for six months. John
Blight was landlord in 1858 followed by Amos Eady and then Richard Lewis.
When Mr. Lewis died in 1866 the licence passed to his widow Susannah
Lewis, who subsequently remarried, her new husband being carpenter
George Morse who took over the running of the pub. He built a carpentry
shop alongside, while in the 1870s the pub also incorporated a small shop
which was run as a branch of Morris Phillips' grocery store in Narberth.

In January 1875 Mr. Frederick Robert Lloyd Child held a housewarming
party to mark his arrival as landlord. The son of the local squire and a skilled
cabinet-maker, he remained until 1879 when he moved to the Castle Inn in
Narberth. At about this time the trustees of the late Thomas Codd, the
Sageston maltster, offered up for sale:

The Begelly Arms public house, cottage and garden and two fields adjoining containing six acres, held on lease for the life of Thomas Evans, now aged 60 years, and subject to the rent of £5.

In the 1880s the Begelly Arms was the registered office of the Begelly Friendly Society which had 79 members. It was also the local base of the Odd Fellows, while the bizarrely named Begelly Tulip Lodge of the British Order of Ancient Free Gardeners had a club room above the public bar. (The lodge later built its own premises — the Free Gardeners' Hall in Kilgetty).

From 1880 to the First World War the licence was held by Alfred Davies, a cabinet-maker, wheelwright and undertaker who had previously worked at the Begelly Arms as a carpenter for George Morse. Mr. Davies made coffins in a workshop adjoining the inn, and owned a four-wheeled horse-drawn hearse — he was also happy to act as the village dentist, charging half-a-crown to pull a tooth. All this must have made him too busy to run the pub, because from 1915 to 1929 his wife Mrs. Elizabeth Davies was the licensee. The Davieses purchased the pub and six acres for £800 in 1919 when the Camrose estate disposed of dozens of properties in the Begelly area; the auction was held at the Begelly Arms. According to Mr. W.R. Morgan:

> The Begelly Arms in the 1920s had a public bar, the floor of which had flag-stones. It had a few hard chairs and a long wooden bench. It was unusual to find more than a few people in the bar because money was scarce.

Thomas Lawrence, who ran the Begelly Arms from 1929 to 1948, was once fined £4 for supplying beer out of hours, the occasion being a Gypsy 'wake' attended by most of the travellers from the nearby Kingsmoor common. Henry White, who took over in 1949, began the process of trans-forming the old pub into the complex which exists today by building a dining room and obtaining a supper licence in 1952. He was followed by Eric Bancroft, while by the time Victor Wood was the landlord from 1966 to 1974 the Begelly Arms had become part of The Crossroads Motel, complete with 16 motel units and a 100-seater restaurant. Teddie George subsequently oversaw the running of the business, acting as licensee/manager, and he was followed by Mr. and Mrs. Austin

An advert for the Begelly Arms in the 1950s when Henry White was licensee.

The Begelly Arms in recent years.

Ollin who were there for 13 years, during which time the motel part of the complex was 'mothballed'. Mr. Ollin — a former AA patrolman — concentrated instead on catering for functions and the Begelly Arms became one of the most popular places in the county for events such as rugby club annual dinners and wedding parties. Mr. and Mrs. John Hogan have been the licensees for the past five years, and are building up the accommodation side of the business once again.

On the corner of the hill leading up to the church was the **Spread Eagle**. Benjamin Protheroe was the landlord from 1822 to 1827 and the pub is shown on a map of 1840 as having a malthouse attached. The name must have changed at some stage, because in February 1851, following the death of Benjamin's widow, Ann, an advert appeared in the local press which read as follows:

> To be let (by direction of the executors of the late Mrs. Protheroe) and entered upon immediately. All that Old Established Inn well known by the name of **Begelly Bottom** in the village of Begelly, with 12 acres or thereabouts of rich meadow and pasture land.

Applicants were informed that the property was well suited for a variety of enterprises. It later became a farm, and after falling derelict a few years ago the building has recently been fully restored.

Colliers employed at the Broom and Thomas Chapel mines would have made the **Miners' Arms** their local; indeed, on Shrove Tuesday, 1827, the Miners' Friendly Society met at the Miners' Arms and enjoyed 'a comfortable dinner which did much credit to the landlord, Mr. Thomas Allen', while nearly 50 years later over 130 coal-workers gathered at the pub and voted in favour of forming themselves into a branch of the Miners' Union.

Thomas Allen appears to have opened the Miners' Arms in 1813 and he remained the landlord until at least 1828. Records are sketchy for the next 30 years, although it is recorded that Philip Harries of the Miners' Arms died in 1839 at the remarkable age of 100. George Teague, the landlord between 1859 and 1874, seems to have been an unusual character. In 1861 he appeared in court charged with mixing Guinea pepper with hops to adulterate his beer. A couple of years later, according to *Potter's Electric News,* he decided to test whether living creatures could survive in extreme conditions underground. Accordingly he buried a toad in a basin covered with a slate for precisely 12 months. 'Then on Saturday last,' reported the newspaper, 'he dug it up and on removing the basin in the presence of some people, to their astonishment the creature was alive and looked as if it had not been there an hour'.

William Powell took over in 1874, while John Bowen was the licensee from 1880 until his death in 1883. He belonged to a family of publicans, and relatives ran the Corporation Arms in Laugharne and the Llwyngwair Arms at Red Roses (now the Sporting Chance). James Bowen applied to take over the licence of the Miners' Arms from his late son, but for some reason this was refused by the magistrates. They turned him down again the following year, and when Stephen Jones took over the tenancy in 1885 and tried to reopen the pub they turned him down as well.

This was the end of the Miners' Arms as a pub. In *The Story of Begelly* (1980), Mr. W.R. Morgan wrote: 'The Miners' Arms has recently been demolished and in its place stands the new Begelly Lodge Hotel'. By the time he came to write *A Pembrokeshire Countryman Looks Back* in 1988, things had moved on: 'A restaurant has been established at the old Miners' Arms, now known as "Miners' Arms II — the Taj Mahal Tandoora Restaurant" '.

There were a couple of ale-houses in the coal-mining area around Thomas Chapel. Farmer Richard Morgan kept the **Lamb** in the 1840s and was fined ten shillings in 1849 for serving beer on a Sunday during church hours. He lived in Thomas Chapel itself, while at Sunnyhill, between Thomas Chapel and Hackett, a widow named Ann Eynon was running an unnamed beer-house at the time of the 1851 census.

CHAPTER THREE

Saundersfoot

According to Mr. T.G. Stickings in *The Story of Saundersfoot*: 'In 1820 there were no more than half a dozen houses and two hostelries in the centre of Saundersfoot'. This was before the rapid development in the late 1820s and early '30s brought about by the increase in coal-mining and other industrial activities in the locality, and the consequent building of the Saundersfoot mineral railway and harbour. Saundersfoot soon became a busy coal-port and an important cog in the British brewing industry, with Pembrokeshire anthracite leaving the harbour in vessels bound for Rochester in Kent (where the coal was used for hop-drying), for the maltings at Snape in Suffolk and for the Guinness brewery in Dublin.

Although the railway eventually took away some of its trade, the little port remained busy for many years, with coastal trading vessels laden with general cargoes joining the coal-boats in the often crowded tidal harbour. The decline in the local coal industry, and in particular the closure of Bonville's Court Colliery in 1930, was offset by a growing tourist trade which is now the main local industry.

The two 1820 'pre-industrial' hostelries mentioned by Mr. Stickings would appear to have been the Milford Arms and the Wogan Arms. Indeed, the **Wogan Arms** in Wogan Terrace is thought by some to be the oldest building in the village. The inn was named in honour of the Wogans, an ancient Pembrokeshire family of landowners whose main estates were at Boulston and Wiston. However the family also occupied the manor and estates of Hean Castle, including much of present-day Saundersfoot, and John Wogan of Hean Castle was Sheriff of Pembrokeshire in 1745.

The first known tenant of the Wogan Arms was Thomas James who was there from 1811 to 1822. In September 1823, William James — probably a son — was considered 'a person of good fame and reputation and of sober life and conversation and a fit and proper person to be entrusted with a licence to the house known by the sign of the Wogan's Arms, lately licensed to Thomas James deceased'. William James was still there in 1858 when he also farmed about 30 acres, but by the time of the 1861 census the innkeeper was his son Thomas James, 26, who ran the inn with the help of his wife Elizabeth.

A mariner named Thomas Beavans was licensee in 1871, while in August 1873 the licence passed to Louis Lillburn, who was still there in 1884. The inn was still open in 1887 but had closed by 1891. It was largely rebuilt soon afterwards and by 1901 Wogan House was being described as 'an ornamental villa of tasteful design'; it is now a guest house.

Apart from the Wogans, the other major landowners in the area were the Philipps family of Picton Castle and, more locally, of Kilgetty House, and it was in their honour that the **Milford Arms** was named; this must have occurred after 1776, in which year the Kilgetty-born Sir Richard Philipps was created Lord Milford. William Ormond is believed to have been the innkeeper from 1784 to 1795, the Milford Arms being part of a long-established and extensive property known as Saundersfoot Farm which was located in the valley behind the beach. In 1818, Thomas Lewis took out a lease on 'part of the farm of Saundersfoot' from the Philipps estate, promising to pay £40 and a bushel of oats annually. Lewis acted as farmer and innkeeper until 1845 when he retired from business at the age of 74.

The Cambrian in 1905.

Following his retirement the Milford Arms was advertised as being to let 'with or without the farm of Saundersfoot comprising 53 acres of good arable, pasture and meadow land'. The new tenant was Thomas Rees, while maltster and brewer Benjamin Jones was in charge from 1851 until 1858. However, both the Milford Arms and Saundersfoot Farm were unoccupied at the time of the 1861 census as the area began to be re-developed with the building of the seaward facing Cambrian Terrace.

The Cambrian as it looked in the early 1970s.

Picture courtesy of the *Western Telegraph*.

This terrace incorporated the **Cambrian**, a purpose-built inn-cum-hotel which evidently replaced the aging Milford Arms and was aimed squarely at the tourist trade being generated by the arrival of the railway in the mid-1860s. John Lewis held the licence of the Cambrian in 1873 and the following year he was convicted of serving after hours. William Llewellyn was there from 1879 to 1884, while the next licensee was William Devereux who was fined ten shillings in 1887 for being drunk and disorderly. W.R. Morgan was landlord by 1891 and the long-serving John Ormond kept the 'Cam' from 1895 to 1931. Captain Jimmy Davies, a yeomanry officer in the First World War, was mine host from 1932 to 1951, followed by Thomas Roblin and later by Albert Harries who provided shark-fishing trips for his more adventurous guests. By this time the Cambrian was a modernised 40-bedroom hotel, having been extended to take in other properties along the terrace. The hotel was badly damaged by a massive gas explosion in October 1984 which demolished the building next door; miraculously, no-one was killed in the blast and despite initial fears that part of it might have to be pulled down, the Cambrian survived and it remains a thriving hostelry.

The Picton Castle inn became the Hean Castle in the 1870s.

One of Saundersfoot's most imposing inns is the **Hean Castle.** This was originally named the **Picton Castle**, again in honour of the landowning Philipps family, and it seems to have opened in the early 1840s. This coincided with the opening of the important colliery at nearby Bonville's Court which was founded in 1840 and began production a couple of years later. In fact, the first licensee appears to have been Bonville's Court colliery agent John Jones, and when in 1846 a new lodge of the Odd Fellows was opened at the Picton Castle, Brother Jones provided a 'sumptuous meal'. The Picton was a solid, four-square building, three storeys high, commanding a view of the seafront. Novelist and travel writer George Borrow is said to have stayed there in 1857 and enjoyed a dip in the nearby sea. Thomas Rees was landlord at the time, perhaps having moved from the Milford Arms, while former Kilgetty colliery agent Richard Hare from Middlesex was landlord between 1858 and 1861.

William Thomas — who also farmed 47 acres — was innkeeper from 1867 until 1881. During his time the inn was extensively remodelled and the name changed from Picton Castle to Hean Castle. This was at the instigation of Charles Ranken Vickerman, a land-owner and industrialist who had become the leading figure in the development of Saundersfoot as a coal-producing and exporting area. Having purchased the Hean Castle estate in 1863 and built the present manor house with its mock gothic towers and crenellations, he then turned his attention to the inn, and in the late 1870s it was converted into the castellated edifice that exists today.

In 1872, William Thomas served 'a most recherche luncheon' between innings when Saundersfoot played Castlemartin at cricket. The game took place in the grounds of Hean Castle, so naturally Charles Vickerman opened the batting in both innings, scoring nought and eight. William Thomas left in 1881 when Joseph Johns took over the licence. A few months later he absconded, so that an advertisement appeared in the *Welshman* newspaper stating that 'the free house known as the Hean Castle inn, the leading hotel in this picturesque and rising watering place' was to be let. Edwin Andrews was the man who took over.

Louis Lillburn became landlord in the early 1890s having moved from the

Men of the King's Shropshire Light Infantry take a break from bicycle patrol to enjoy refreshments at the Hean Castle.

Picture courtesy of Mr. Gary Davies.

Wogan Arms around the corner; he was also the local harbour-master. In 1898 it was reported that the Hean was being taken over by Mr. Fred Cole 'who is thoroughly fitting it out and making it quite an up-to-date establishment'. He was keen to attract commercial travellers to the inn, but wasn't there for long because Mrs. Annie Rees held the licence in 1899. Mrs. Elizabeth Hughes was the landlady from 1904 to 1907 and Bill Thomas was licensee before the First World War. Emily Thomas took over in 1914 and left in 1921, while William Sabin was the licensee in 1924. When he went bankrupt the licence passed to George Waldron from Birmingham who was still there in 1936. Mrs. Mary Jane Waldron then ran the Hean from 1936 to 1943, followed by Elizabeth Lomas and Dilys Williams.

The Hean Castle, Saundersfoot,
as it looked in 2002.

The Hean was purchased in about 1960 by Mr. Wyndham Evans (son of Jack Evans of the Fountain Head) who carried out some much-needed repairs and internal alterations to the old building. Mr. Evans employed George Derbyshire as manager to run the business, but in 1965 the inn was sold to Mr. Eric Caine. When Mr. Caine left in the early 1970s — coincidentally to run the Fountain Head — the management of the Hean passed to his son Maurice, and later to his other son Peter who stayed until 1988. Mr. Peter Caine still owns the Hean but he now runs the Old Chemist inn just round the corner and the Hean has been leased out; licensee for the past 13 years has been David Lloyd.

The pleasantly traditional **Royal Oak** in Wogan Terrace was kept by Thomas Ormond from Martletwy between 1837 and 1852 when the lease of the inn was advertised as being available because the licensee intended emigrating to Australia. The inn was described as having excellent stables, brewhouse, gardens and other offices. However, Mr. Ormond must have had second thoughts about migrating, because he stayed in Saundersfoot and carried on running the Royal Oak until 1873. He handed on to Samuel Lewis who remained landlord until his death in 1878. Sarah Lewis took over, followed by Eliza Mary Lewis; at this time the Oak was the favourite watering hole of the sea captains whose vessels traded at Saundersfoot harbour.

The licensee from 1882 to 1886 was John Thomas, who was regularly in trouble for being drunk behind the bar, and W.G. Llewellyn held the licence in 1887. He was followed by Mrs. Sarah Thomas who was landlady

A recent view of the Royal Oak.

from 1891 to 1900. The landlord from 1901 to 1910 was Charles Davies who arrived from Wiston and departed to live in Canada. Edward Cramond took over, but his tenure ended tragically in 1913 when he committed suicide at the back of the pub by cutting his throat. He had been suffering from depression caused by money difficulties. William Bodill was there during the First World War followed by Lillian Wickham — later Mrs. Lillian Richards.

In 1922 the pub was put up for auction, the sale particulars stating that it possessed a bar, commercial room, parlour, two kitchens, scullery, six bedrooms and a stable. Uri Jones from Pentre, Glamorgan, was the top bidder with £375 and a few months later Joseph Jones took over the running of the pub. Gilead Spencer Einon replaced him in 1927 and his name was still over the door in the 1950s. Like the Hean Castle, the Royal Oak was subsequently purchased and refurbished by Mr. Wyndham Evans before being leased out, and it remains his property. The licensee in the 1980s and for much of the '90s was Robbie Jones and the present landlord is Mr. Trevor Suter.

The **Brewery Tap** was evidently part of the fairly extensive Saundersfoot Brewery which Thomas Stephenson established in the 1840s. The original brewery building collapsed one night in 1852 as a result of the foundations being undermined by workmen who had been employed to excavate a series of cellars. The premises were rebuilt, and in 1855, an advert in the local press described the business as 'an ale and porter

Saundersfoot brewery in the 1890s.
Picture courtesy of Mr. Roscoe Howells.

brewery with small steam engine, malthouse and granary'. It added: 'A Tap attached more than clears the whole of the working expenses'.

It appears that the running of the brewery and the licence of the Brewery Tap then passed to Benjamin Thomas, a local tradesman who was involved in a couple of other local pubs as well as various business ventures. However he nearly ended up in prison following an incident in the 1860s when two local police officers attempted to enter the Brewery Tap in order to arrest a female felon. Landlord Thomas was somewhat drunk at the time and not only refused admission to the worthy constables but assaulted the pair of them for good measure. At the local Petty Sessions, Thomas was ordered to pay £5 plus 17 shillings costs, the alternative being four months' imprisonment with hard labour.

An early postcard view of Railway Street (now the Strand) in Saundersfoot.

Daniel Davies, formerly of the Fountain Head, ran the Brewery Tap for a few years while Benjamin Thomas involved himself in his other businesses, but by October 1877 Thomas was back at the Brewery Tap where he stayed until 1884. In 1886 the licence was being held by John Pugh who lived at the Prince of Wales in Tenby; he installed Martha Pugh as manageress of the 'Tap'. The pub — though not the brewery — was still going in 1891 when blacksmith Evan Phillips was the landlord, but it seems to have closed soon afterwards; it was located in what is still known as Brewery Terrace.

There is a local tradition that the **Square and Compass** was at the southern end of Railway Street (now The Strand), and that it was one of the first buildings to be erected as the tiny hamlet began to be transformed into a coal-exporting port. At some stage the **Drapers' Arms** was opened on the site of the old 'Square' by the aforementioned Benjamin Thomas who ran the pub in the early 1870s while his wife Louisa ran the drapery side of the business. In October 1877, when the Thomases moved to live above the Brewery Tap, the licence passed to George Green, while chemist David Lewis was the new tenant and licensee in 1880. The pub closed in the 1880s and by 1901 it had become the village post office.

Interestingly, it appears that several licensed premises in Saundersfoot, notably the Drapers' Arms, the Wogan Arms and the Brewery Tap, closed in the late 1880s and early 1890s. This may have had something to do with the growing temperance movement in the little port and particularly the opening of the Evelyn Coffee Tavern in High Street in 1886, which provided the miners and seamen with a sober alternative to the pot-houses of the town.

Thomas Mathias, druggist, grocer and seedsman, was landlord of the **Globe** in Railway Street from the 1860s to 1892 and the building had a split personality, with a chemist's shop fronting the street while the back room served as a tiny inn. This was a common arrangement; chemists needed a spirit licence to sell certain patent medicines and many capitalised on the fact by running a small pub as a sideline. In 1872, Narberth magistrates threatened to take away Mr. Mathias' licence unless he completely sealed off the pub from the chemist's shop. He did so, and thereafter, beer for the pub had to be delivered by cart along the beach. Mary Mathias was licensee from 1895 to 1900, after which Arthur David Griffiths — who had been taken on by Mr. Mathias as his assistant in 1891 — succeeded to the many-faceted business and ran it until 1940.

Gwynfor Evans took over the Globe in the 1940s and was still there in 1962 by which time Railway Street had become The Strand. When a new chemist's shop was built in the village in the late 1960s, the Globe became

*Delivering beer along the beach to the Globe inn at the back
of the chemist shop in Railway Street.*

Picture courtesy of Mr. Roscoe Howells.

*The present sign of the Old
Chemist in Saundersfoot.*

a pub throughout, the **Old Chemist**, complete with trendy 'cellar bar'. 'A unique feature of this bar is that it leads straight on to the beach via a most attractive and unusual patio designed authentically in Spanish style,' declared a 1970s guide. Mike Timmins was landlord in the early 1970s, after which the pub was purchased by Mr. Peter Caine of the Hean Castle. The 'Chemist' was then managed by Roger Stanford for a while and later leased to Brian Davies, but Mr. Caine has run the pub himself since 1988.

There are references to a 'rail-road' in the Saundersfoot area as early as 1825, and the name **Railway Tavern** appears in the Picton estate papers of about that time. This may have been in the Coppet Hall area, and was almost certainly a different place from the **Railway Inn** which stood near the foot of the old incline tramway. This 'self-acting' incline linked the harbour railway with the coal mines to the west of Saundersfoot — a system which was not in place until the 1830s.

34

Information about the early history of the pub is sketchy, but it seems to have been kept by a mason named William Phillips from about 1840 to 1850. In 1866 the Railway Inn was the scene of an inquest into the death of William Parsell, chief engine man at nearby Bonville's Court colliery. Farrier John Thomas was landlord at the time, and he was still there in 1879 when he handed over to coal miner Rees Davies who still held the licence in 1891. William Davies took over and kept the pub until 1894, but it closed shortly afterwards and is now Railway Inn cottage.

A newspaper report of 1868 referred to a Mrs. Williams of the **Mariners' Inn**, Saundersfoot. Presumably this was the pub which

The former Railway Inn near the foot of the incline.

The Captain's Cabin in the late 1960s.

Picture courtesy of the *Western Telegraph*.

35

Thomas Williams and wife Susan were running near the bottom of St. Bride's Hill at the time of the 1871 census, but about which nothing more is known.

The gabled building known as St. Issells House on the harbour was turned into a restaurant in the 1960s by single-handed transatlantic yachtsman Val Howells. He called it 'The Captain's Table', but by the 1970s it was being run by Bill and Joyce Turner as a pub called **The Captain's Cabin**. Very popular, especially with young people in the summer, it remained a pub until 1995 when the name reverted to 'The Captain's Table' and the restaurant side of the business once more predominated.

CHAPTER FOUR

Kilgetty to Llanteg

In 1866 the railway line from Tenby to Whitland was built, crossing the old mail coach road at a point half a mile east of Begelly. A new station complex with sidings and cattle pens was constructed at this convenient point, the halt being named 'Kilgetty' after a nearby manor house. Soon, a new community began to develop around the station where previously there had been open moorland with just a scattering of farms and miners' cottages.

The **Kilgetty Arms** at the bottom of Ryelands Lane opened soon after the arrival of the railway, and Evan Thomas held the licence in 1867. He was followed by John Mansell who also farmed 20 acres of land near the pub. Benjamin John, who was licensee off and on from 1874 to 1899, held the post of village stationmaster for a time. John Lewis was the landlord from 1900 to 1907 followed by William Scourfield and then John John. Mrs. Sophia John was the landlady from 1917 to 1928 when the licence passed to her son William; 'I am getting too old,' she explained to the magistrates, who courteously replied that she didn't look it.

William John handed over to Billy Griffin in 1944 and William Patterson was there in 1954. Ronnie Ebsworth was the landlord in the early 1960s, followed by Bernie McCarrick who held the licence for over 20 years. The Kilgetty Arms was always busy on mart days, especially after 1924 when it was allowed to remain open throughout the day when the mart-ground next to the station was in operation. However the mart is no longer functioning, and the pub finally closed in the late 1990s; it has since been converted into private accommodation. The last licensee was Stephen Watkins who moved down the road to take over the other village pub.

This was originally called the **Railway**, and Thomas Harries was the landlord between 1869 and 1879 followed by David Thomas who ran the pub in the 1880s. John Merriman — like so many of the Merriman family a blacksmith by trade — was landlord in the 1890s and reputedly specialised in shoeing pit-ponies. William Adams kept the pub from 1899 to 1922, while in 1925 the

The last days of the Kilgetty Arms in the late 1990s.

Photo courtesy of Mr. Gary Davies.

The Railway Inn, Kilgetty, as it looked in the 1920s.

Photo courtesy of Mr. Ken Daniels.

licence passed to Thomas Prosser and he remained the landlord until his death in January 1937. John Crew then ran the Railway for a dozen years, followed by Norman James in the 1950s and Billy Buchan in the 1960s. It was Mr. Buchan who changed the name of the pub in the mid-1960s. He called it the **White Horse**, the name recalling John Merriman's old smithy next door — and also reflecting Mr. Buchan's admiration for the national drink of his native Scotland. The old inn was also given a major refurbishment by the Felinfoel brewery at around this time, the new look being big on horse-shoes and horse-brasses. The White Horse has changed hands several times since Mr. Buchan left, but it remains a popular village social centre.

From iron horse to White Horse —
a change of name for the former Railway Inn.

The former coal-mining and iron-producing village of Stepaside has had a great many ale-houses in its day, and may well have derived its name from an early cottage ale-house — the 'Step Aside' — now long forgotten. Tradition has it that there was also a pub here at one time called the **Camomile Back Inn**, while it is known that coal-miner Charles Absalom ran a pub in the village from 1784 to about 1800.

Several of the early ale-houses were situated just off the old road that led up from Stepaside towards Templeton and Ludchurch, where there was plenty of passing trade from carters of coal and lime as well as a resident population of thirsty mineworkers to keep them busy. The **Square and Compass** was located on the opposite side of the road from the old school and may have been opened by a stonemason from the nearby quarry. John David was the landlord from 1822 to 1828, but the pub seems to have closed by 1841 when the building was simply known as 'The Square'. (In later years it was the family home of the actor Kenneth Griffith). Also in this area was the **Angel** which was kept by Stephen and Mary Griffiths from 1822 to 1851 and by Thomas and Ann Harries in 1861. There is a local tradition that the building now known as Slate Mill Cottage once contained an ale-house, in which case the Angel would appear to fit the bill.

Two other pub names can be found on the 1841 census, the **Victoria Inn** run by William John and the **Kilgetty Arms** run by colliery agent Samuel Singleton. Both appear to have been located somewhere around the Lower Level area of Stepaside and both seem to have been short-lived affairs. The census also mentions a publican by the name of Elizabeth Morgan who lived at Kilvelgy Wells.

These early ale-houses were largely superseded by the **Prince of Wales** which opened in the early 1840s, taking its name from Queen Victoria's first son, Prince Edward. The Prince of Wales was in the heart of Stepaside, and was purpose-built alongside the new mail coach road which sliced through the village in the late 1830s. The first licensees were John and Ann Griffiths who had previously run the Poyer's Arms at Longstone, and they were still at the Prince of Wales in 1861. Robert Hodge, son of Bridget Hodge of the Wiseman's Bridge inn, held the licence in 1871, but the licence passed from him to Margaret Thomas in September 1876 and she ran the pub for the next four years. Warren Collins Williams, a native of Cheltenham, took over in 1880 and was fined 20 shillings in 1882 for being drunk in his own licensed

The Prince of Wales in Stepaside closed some 50 years ago.

premises. He was fined again in 1883 for being drunk and disorderly in the village street, which caused the magistrates to ponder whether he was the right sort of man to be running a pub.

William Absalom held the licence in 1884 and Mrs. Martha Absalom was the licensee from 1895 to 1906. William Richards took over and kept the pub until 1922,

40

working at Bonville's Court colliery during the day; at this time the pub had a tap-room, kitchen, cellar and three bedrooms. John Callen of Saundersfoot successfully bid £595 for the freehold of the pub in 1922 and William Callen was the landlord from 1923 to 1936 when Elizabeth Annie Callen took over the licence. She became Mrs. Lewis in 1938 and remained at the Prince of Wales until 1951, in which year no application was made for the renewal of the pub licence. It has been a private house ever since.

Blacksmith Benjamin Allen from Amroth and his wife Elizabeth kept the **Miners' Arms** in Stepaside in 1851, but nothing else is recorded until 1875 when the licence passed from the new owner of the property, Benjamin Thomas of the brewery in Saundersfoot, to coalminer William Absalom. According to Mr. Roscoe Howells in his book *Old Saundersfoot*, quarry workers from the Ludchurch area would regularly troop down to 'The Pan', as the Miners' Arms was known (being short for 'Pan and Handle'), looking to pick a scrap with the colliers. 'If the old timers are to be believed, they would have made today's football hooligans look like velvet-suited mamma's darlings drinking lemonade at the Sunday school party', observed Mr. Howells.

Certainly the three policemen who were called to a disturbance at the pub in June 1876 were amazed at the riot going on, with the floor littered with over-turned chairs and broken glass and people climbing through the windows to escape the drunken brawl. They were even more surprised to find that the three biggest troublemakers were the landlord William Absalom and his two sons John and Charles, all of them fighting drunk. All three were later fined for drunkenness and assault. (Ironically, a Friendly Society called the Kilgetty United Brotherhood used the alehouse as a base in the 1880s).

Mr. Absalom and his wife Martha ran the Miners' Arms until 1883 when the pub was taken over by William and Elizabeth Allen while the Absaloms moved to the nearby Prince of Wales. The Allens remained until 1923 when the Miners' Arms was forced to close under the redundancy ruling, with £200 in compensation being paid out, mainly to the owner, Sir Charles Philipps. Mrs. Elizabeth Allen was running the pub on her own by this time, her husband William having died in 1907. Mrs. Allen was greatly upset at the

The former Miners' Arms in Stepaside was usually called 'The Pan and Handle'.

41

The former Golden Grove inn looks down on the old iron works.

The present Stepaside inn was opened in a building which once housed the manager of the local iron works.

magistrates' decision to close the business which had been her life for 40 years and she died just a few months after the pub closed. She was 78.

On the opposite side of Pleasant Valley was the **Golden Grove** inn which overlooked the iron-works. Opened in 1849, these iron-works included two blast furnaces, coke ovens and workshops, and used ore mined from the cliffs near Wiseman's Bridge to produce iron for use in local foundries and for export. Collier William Thomas ran the Golden Grove inn from about 1850 to 1863, while George Lewis was landlord in 1867. William Gwyther, who married into the Lewis family, was landlord in the 1870s, but the iron-works closed in 1877 and the pub seems to have closed soon after-wards. The building can still be seen, in the trees above the exten-sive remains of the blast furnaces.

As the area began to embrace tourism in the 1960s, the **Stepaside Inn** was opened in Kilgetty House, at one time the impressive home of the manager of the iron-works. It was extended in the early 1990s to incorporate a large dining area and has since become much less of a pub and more of a restaurant. Licensee for the past eight years or so has been Rob Hill.

Further along the old mail coach road, the pair of semi-detached houses a mile or so east of Stepaside was once the **Cambrian Inn.** This was the home of a coalminer and haulier named Richard Howells — great grandfather of local historian and novelist Mr. Roscoe Howells who explained in his book *Old Saundersfoot*:

> He drove the stones to make the section of the road from Begelly Cross to the county boundary at Castle Ely bridge when the new road was built to improve the approaches to Pembroke Dock harbour in 1837. He had a licence, mainly for supplying beer to the men working for him on the road, and some of the census returns and other records show him described occasionally as inn-keeper, and the Cambrian referred to variously as Cambrian Inn or Cambrian Mailway.

When Richard Howells moved out in the 1850s the licence lapsed. The Cambrian was eventually rebuilt by Mr. Howells' father in about 1930 as a pair of houses called Cambrian Cottages.

Half a mile further along, near the Kilanow toll-gate, was the **Commercial Inn**. George Davies was farming at Little Kilanow in the 1830s, perhaps selling home-brewed beer to passers-by. But when the mail coach road was constructed it by-passed his farm, so he decided to build a new farm-cum-public house alongside the new road. The Commercial was up and running by 1847 and Mr. Davies remained as licensee for half a century; during his long tenure the ownership of the pub passed from the Picton estate to Mr. Samuel Kay of Colby Lodge. Mr. Davies, who was also the local registrar of births, marriages and deaths, was succeeded in 1897 by his widow Martha Davies who kept the pub for half a dozen years, while from 1904 until his death in 1936 the licensee was John Friend. Mr. Friend obviously liked a drink himself, and he was severely reprimanded by the magistrates in 1918 after being convicted on two separate occasions for being drunk and disorderly and drunk in charge of a pony and cart.

The Commercial at Kilanow became the Stage Coach in 1965 but has since closed.

Thomas Lewis was landlord from 1937 to 1954, after which Alistair 'Jock' Murdoch purchased the inn and 28 acres from the Colby Estate. At the time the inn consisted of two public rooms — a bar and a tiny lounge — and was without electricity or running water. Mr. and Mrs. Murdoch carried out a great number of improvements during the course of their 34 years in charge, and they also changed the name to the **Stage Coach** in 1965. As the only real social centre for many miles around, the Stage Coach had a big local following, especially on Saturday nights when the L-shaped bar was invariably packed. When the Murdochs retired, the pub was run for several years by Richard and Janet Finch, but it is now a private house.

To the north of Telford's road is the parish of Ludchurch — a scattering of farms, cottages and quarries roughly centred on the Norman church of St. Elidyr. For the past 50 years this widespread community has come under one umbrella and has been known as Ludchurch village, but prior to that the tiny hamlets of Longstone, Egypt and Blaencilgoed each had its own separate identity — and its own ale-houses.

The area has long been renowned for its limestone quarries, the stone being used for building purposes and also burned in kilns to provide lime to 'sweeten' the fields. Coal was carted to the kilns from the pits around Stepaside, while farmers from a wide area travelled to Ludchurch to collect the lime. The heavy tolls exacted on these lime-carts by the various turnpike trusts were a constant source of irritation which eventually boiled over to become one of the causes of the Rebecca Riots. The main quarries were in Egypt — where the stone was quarried right up to the churchyard wall — and at Blaencilgoed to the east.

There was one ale-house in the parish in 1784, run by Thomas James, while Thomas Evans ran the solitary ale-house in 1795. As quarrying increased in the 1820s, so did the number of places offering refreshment to the thirsty quarrymen, lime-burners and carters. One of these was the **Poyer's Arms** where John Child was the licensee from 1823 to 1831. This pub was in the Longstone area, near Kings Park, and the name is thought to have derived from the fact that the property was owned by Mr. Charles Poyer Callen, a local coal-owner who was related to the land-owning Poyer family of Grove near Narberth. John and Anne Griffiths were the licensees in 1841, but they moved to the Prince of Wales in Stepaside during the 1840s when the Poyer's Arms must have closed.

Mr. A. Eric Evans, in his well-researched book *Our Village — A History of Ludchurch*, recorded that a cooper named William Murray was running the **Square and Compass**, Egypt, at the time when the 1836 voters list was compiled. The name would have appealed to the stonemasons from the nearby quarries but the pub seems to have been a short-lived venture. Mr. Evans thought that the Square and Compass was in the building now known as 'The Cottage'.

The **White Horse** in Egypt was recorded between 1822 and 1827 when David Williams was the landlord. It seems to have been one of two adjoining cottages, the other one being an ale-house at a much later stage. The two cottages stood on the site of what is now a private house known as Ceffyl Lwyd.

The later ale-house presents some problems, because while the name on the sign was apparently **Golden Lion**, everyone seems to have called it by the name of the cottage which was the **Grey Horse**. So while John Thomas of the Grey Horse, Ludchurch was mentioned in the *Welshman* newspaper of February 1882, the 1881 census shows him living at the Golden Lion, Ludchurch. Recalling her Victorian childhood in Ludchurch, Mrs. T.R. Lawrence of Westerton Farm wrote in 1968: 'There were two public houses in the parish, one at Grey Horse and Ludchurch Farm. Home brewed'.

Ludchurch Farm at the heart of Egypt was the location of the last surviving ale-house in the parish, the **Limekiln**, where the innkeeper from 1867 onwards was George Watkins. He was also a farmer on a fairly substantial scale and employed eight men and one boy on the 230-acre farm in 1881. The farm still comprises a large number of buildings, and it is impossible to be certain which of them housed the pub which closed following George Watkins' death in about 1884. His widow subsequently put the farm up for auction, the sale particulars noting that there was 'a valuable limestone quarry on the farm' as well as 'a vein of silica clay and sand running from the surface to a great depth'. Some people have suggested that it was this supply of sand which gave the area its

Oaklands near Llanteg was once the Royal Oak.

name of Egypt; a more likely explanation is that it was a long-standing campsite rendezvous for Gypsies.

To the north of the village near Ludchurch Cross was the **Star**, which is thought to have closed during the middle of the 19th century and which is now Croft Farm. Benjamin David opened a pub here in 1828, while Benjamin Edwards and wife Sarah were the licensees in 1841.

Returning to Telford's turnpike, there were a couple more roadside inns which opened in the 1830s to serve the navvies building the road

This roadside building in Llanteg, pictured in 2003, was twice a public house — the Golden Lion in the 1840s and The Laurels in the 1890s.

and which remained open for a few years afterwards in the hope of making a living from the passing trade. One of these was the **Royal Oak** which stood a little to the west of the village of Llanteg on the Ludchurch side of the road. Jane Griffiths was the publican in 1841, and according to the census she was just 16 years old. In 1844 the Loyal Tudor lodge of Odd Fellows met here before processing to Amroth Church for a service, but it had become a farm called The Oakland by 1851. It is now Oaklands, a private house set back from the road following one of the many realignments of the original carriageway.

Further along and on the opposite side of the road in Llanteg itself was the **Golden Lion**. This was kept in 1841 by Allan Palmer who appears to have been a butcher as well. Like the Royal Oak it had closed by the end of the decade,

Benfro bitter was once brewed at Llanteglos.

and Llanteg drinkers thereafter were obliged to travel further afield, or else had to resort to shebeens such as that run by Anne Morgans in the 1850s. In 1898, Mr. W.W. Williams reopened the Golden Lion as a pub under the new name of **The Laurels**. However it only remained open for a few years and by 1902 had once again become a private house; it is still known to this day as The Laurels.

Two other pubs in the Llanteg area, separated by several hundred years, are the long-forgotten **New Inn** which was recorded in 1712 and the recent **Wanderer's Rest** at Llanteglos. It was at the Llanteglos holiday site that Mr. Peter Johnson set up a micro-brewery in 1985 to produce his own Benfro range of Pembrokeshire beers. After enjoying considerable initial success, the brewery ran into distribution problems and ceased brewing in 1990.

CHAPTER FIVE

Amroth to Wiseman's Bridge

The coastal village of Amroth on the Carmarthenshire border is divided into three distinct settlements, one at either end of a windswept sand-and-pebble beach and a third, much older community alongside the church of St. Elidyr on a wooded hill behind. Below the church is Amroth Castle, a manor house formerly known as Earwear Mansion, which was rebuilt in its present castellated form in about 1800.

The western part of Amroth began to develop in the first half of the 19th century as a result of small-scale coal and iron mining. The coal was excavated in pits scattered along the valley behind The Burrows (as this settlement was known), although there were also a couple of workings close to the entrance to Amroth Castle. The iron ore was worked in 'patches' along the sea-cliffs between Amroth and Wiseman's Bridge, the raw mineral being transported to the iron-works at Stepaside. While few traces of the coal workings remain, the rockfalls and spoil-heaps along the shoreline to the west are a lasting indication of the former iron 'patches'.

Amroth, and particularly The Burrows, has had a long and stormy relationship with the sea. A row of five cottages was swept away in the 1930s and massive coastal defences have been erected in recent years to try to keep the storms at bay. It is the wide stretch of beach which makes Amroth popular with summer visitors, and they, in their turn, have contributed in great measure to keeping open the three village pubs.

The oldest of these is the **New Inn** which stands alongside the stream which once formed the boundary with Carmarthenshire and which is traditionally the start — or finish — of the Pembrokeshire National Park's long-distance coastal footpath. The coast road which passes the inn was once the shortest route between Swansea and Tenby, via rowing-boat ferries at Llansteffan and Laugharne. However, it was rarely the quickest option, the bridle-way being badly surfaced and sometimes impassable. To make matters worse, the lonely track between Pendine and the New Inn was 'calculated for

The building on the left is the New Inn, separated from the sea by a pebble bank in this early 20th-century view.

Picture courtesy of Mr. Gary Davies.

plunder, strategems and murder' according to *The Cambrian Tourist or Post-Chaise Companion* — a sort of early 19th century *Rough Guide to Wales*. Explaining that the area around Green Bridge was 'infested by an unawed banditti of smugglers', the author of *The Cambrian Tourist*, the Rev. G.R. Whittaker, advised travellers heading towards Tenby to take an inland route instead.

Those who disregarded his advice found little to cheer them. J.T. Barber, writing in 1803, recorded that he entered Pembrokeshire 'at a place called New Inn'. He depicted it as 'a small collection of cottages on the beach with a large old mansion lately modernised'. The inn may have been closed at this stage, because he could find 'no house of public entertainment as the name would imply'. Likewise, E. Donovan, who passed this way a couple of years later, was warned that New Inn was 'a miserable village destitute of any house of public accommodation'.

Perhaps the inn was so small and hidden away that the early travellers didn't notice it. Certainly the New Inn was up and running in the 1830s, when William Lewis was the landlord, also farming 302 acres 'and 107 acres of mountain' with the help of his sons Griff and John. In 1853 the New Inn was badly hit by flooding — not for the last time. Everything in the garden was washed away, including a cart which was later found on Tenby sands. William Lewis remained in charge until the 1860s, while the landlord in 1875 was William Williams from Marros. He was followed by his widow Margaret

A recent view of the New Inn, which is now in Pembrokeshire thanks to a tweaking of the border.

in 1881 and their daughter and son-in-law Martha and William Richards ran the pub in 1891.

John Davies took over in about 1894 and was still in charge in 1939. The pub nearly had to close in March 1928 following police objections to the renewal of the licence on the grounds that the New Inn wasn't 'necessary'. Whitland magistrates were told by a police sergeant that Mr. Davies only sold two gallons of beer a week, a bottle of spirits a month and six bottles of stout a week, so closing the pub would be no hardship to anyone.

Conceding that Mr. Davies had never been convicted of any mis-demeanour, P.S. Thomas continued: 'The sanitary conditions are generally poor, there is no provision for supplying the public with refreshments other than intoxicants, and there is no sleeping accommodation'. He felt that Amroth people were adequately served by the Temple Bar and the Amroth Arms, while the Green Bridge was only a couple of miles in the other direction.

Mr. Davies agreed that he only had six or seven customers a week in the depth of winter and that the place was a little dilapidated, but he added that the pub provided a valuable service at other times of the year, especially as that end of the beach was very popular with motorists and picnic parties. 'We regularly boil water for Sunday School parties to have tea on the beach', he added. This last fact must have impressed the magistrates, because to the surprise of most people in the courtroom they decided to allow Mr. Davies to keep his licence.

In the 1950s the New Inn was run by Ena Bodimead, and John Morgan was landlord in the 1960s, the pub being gradually upgraded to meet the demands of a growing numbers of tourists. Paul and Kathryn Luger took over in 1975 and ran the pub for over 20 years; the licence then passed to their son — also Paul — and he is still the landlord. Being at one time a yard or two on the Carmarthenshire side of the county border, the New Inn was dry on Sundays for several years while the other two village pubs, being both in 'wet' Pembrokeshire, were allowed to serve on the Sabbath. Eventually Carmarthenshire also became 'wet' on Sundays, but, rather ironically, thanks to a recent change in the county boundary the New Inn is now officially within Pembrokeshire.

The original Amroth Arms, sometimes known as the Amroth Castle Arms, which stood near the castle entrance.
Picture courtesy of Mr. Roscoe Howells.

Between the New Inn and the entrance to the castle was the original **Amroth Arms,** sometimes known as the **Amroth Castle Arms**. This was the home of joiner George Child from 1841 to 1851 and tailor and publican Henry Lewis in 1861. The licence was subsequently transferred to the present Amroth Arms, while the original building was eventually pulled down on the orders of Lord Kylsant, apparently to allow his new motor-car an unimpeded passage through the gates of Amroth Castle.

The new **Amroth Arms** was built by local grocer and property developer Thomas Lewis in about 1870. He ran the pub himself for a year or two, but then decided to move on. In October 1873 the *Welshman* newspaper reported: 'A capitally-built public house called the Amroth Arms has been recently erected and is well adapted for an innkeeper's business'. The following year Mr. Lewis handed over to William Ebsworth — the first of several Ebsworths to enter the licensing trade — but he died a couple of years afterwards and

The present Amroth Arms as it looked in about 1906.
Picture courtesy of Mr. Gary Davies.

the licence passed to Thomas Phelps. James Beynon, a farm labourer from over the border in Marros, was running the place by 1881, and he was still there in 1919 having survived the battering of the great storms of 1896 when the pub was swamped by the sea.

From 1920 until his death in 1932 William James held the licence, and from 1933 to 1941 the licensees were Mr. and Mrs. Edgar Newman. In 1944 the licence passed from the late Mr. Frederick Butler to his daughter Mrs. Margaret Baker who ran the inn until 1953. Ruth Speight was there in the 1950s, while George Torkington, who held the licence from 1958 into the early 1960s, began the task of modernising the pub to cater for the tourist trade. He employed managers to run the business and also opened a sea-food restaurant which specialised in lobster — earning the Amroth Arms the nick-name 'The Lobster Pub'.

Noel Davies was the landlord in the late 1960s, and he was followed in 1971 by the present licensee, Roger Harries. It was Mr. Harries who completed the refurbishment of the inn, opening up the building and combining under one roof the two adjoining premises which previously made up the pub. An old flight of stairs was removed from the building during these

51

The original front door of the Amroth Arms had become a window by 1968.
Picture courtesy of the *Western Telegraph.*

*The Amroth Arms had been extended and modernised by the time
this 2001 photograph was taken.*

alterations; even so, on dark winter nights, footsteps can still be heard climbing and descending the staircase that is no longer there ....

The name 'Temple Bar' can be found in Amroth on a map of 1773 at The Burrows end of the beach. Where the name came from is open to debate, but one possible theory is that it refers to a long sand-bar just offshore, with the 'Temple' part of the name coming from the Order of Templars which owned lands in the area. It has also been suggested that 'Temple Bar' could have been a nickname for a local toll-gate.

When the coal-mining Thomas family built a string of properties at The Burrows in the 1840s, John Thomas opened one of them as a pub which he called the **Temple Bar**. He remained landlord from 1851 to 1877, being followed by his widow Maria Thomas who was there until 1896. She catered for meetings of the Amroth Burrows Friendly Society whose 34 members made the pub their registered office. Another John Thomas — presumably a son of the previous licensees — took over in 1896 and remained in charge until his death in 1900, after which the landlady until 1914 was Mrs. Mary Thomas. During her time an Amroth village band was formed and made its headquarters at the Temple Bar. Oddly enough, the band was closely connected with the Band of Hope temperance movement — a clash of interests which, as Mr. Roscoe Howells has pointed out, 'possibly explains why its activities were short-lived'.

The Thomas family connection ended when Thomas Ebsworth took over in 1915, but the pub came within a whisker of being closed by the magistrates

This superb postcard shows the Temple Bar in Amroth in Edwardian times, with a party of fashionably-dressed ladies apparently waiting for their menfolk to emerge from the pub so that they can continue their Sunday carriage outing.

Picture courtesy of Mr. Gary Davies.

in 1917 after the licensee was convicted of serving after hours — regarded as a heinous crime during the war years. The licence was eventually renewed on appeal, allowing Mr. Ebsworth to carry on running the pub until the Second World War (he purchased the freehold of the building for £500 at an auction in 1922). Mrs. Elizabeth Ebsworth took over in 1942 and was still in charge through the 1950s.

The Temple Bar inn as it appears today — drastically altered from the way it looked a century earlier.

When the Ebsworths were there, the Temple Bar was a small, old-fashioned village pub with a bar-room to the right of the front door and a small parlour on the left, but it has since been changed beyond all recognition to cater for the influx of summer tourists. It was local builder Mr. Billy Lewis who was responsible for this transformation in the early 1970s, and he subsequently ran the pub with his wife Valma for several years. The Temple Bar is still being run by members of the Lewis family, so that each of the three surviving pubs in the village has remained in the same hands for some 30 years — an unusual occurrence made more remarkable by the fact that each of the families has a strong German connection.

In the 1790s, Thomas Prout kept an ale-house in the area of what is now Summerhill. This was the **Fox and Hounds**, usually referred to locally as 'Foxenholes'. Another early pub in Amroth parish was the **New Tavern.** In 1815, William Edwards, mariner, and his wife Sarah were living at the New Tavern, but nothing further is known.

At the height of the local mineral industry there were a couple of ale-houses between Amroth and Wiseman's Bridge. Elizabeth Griffiths and her coal-miner husband Joseph kept a pub on Duncow Hill from 1841 to 1851, in which year it was named in the census as the **Miners' Arms**. Joseph and Elizabeth were committed to the Mormon cause, which was surprisingly strong in the Amroth area at the time, and in 1853 — when both were in their 60s — they left the Miners' Arms with several other members of their family to join the Mormon community at Salt Lake City in Utah. A five-week sea crossing to New Orleans was followed by a steamer journey up the Mississippi and a wagon train trek across the prairies to Utah. Elizabeth didn't make it to the Promised Land; she died during the wagon journey and was buried alongside the trail. But Joseph and the rest of the family completed the epic journey from the Miners' Arms to Salt Lake City, and their fascinating tale is told at much greater length in *From Amroth to Utah* by Mr. Roscoe Howells. Coincidentally, it was Mr. Howells' great grand-father Richard Howells who replaced Joseph and Elizabeth Griffiths at the Miners' Arms, having moved from the Cambrian Inn outside Stepaside. Whether he continued to run it as an ale-house isn't known, however.

The long-demolished New Alehouse on Duncow Hill with what looks to be a fairly substantial malthouse on the right.

Picture courtesy of Mr. Gary Davies.

The **New Alehouse**, which stood near the bottom of Duncow Hill, was a cottage inn known locally as 'The New Al'us'. When it was in operation isn't clear; the earliest recorded reference is 1822, while none of the people who lived there when the census enumerator came to call ever admitted to being an ale-house keeper. It was certainly defunct by 1870.

The **Wiseman's Bridge Inn** is now popular with tourists, but it was once at the heart of the local coal and iron industry. Before the building of Saundersfoot Harbour, coal was transported to Wiseman's Bridge by ox-cart

A lady cyclist adjusts her impressive hat in front of the Wiseman's Bridge Inn.

and loaded onto vessels beached on the shore. This was thirsty work and there must have been a pub hereabouts from an early date; certainly Jane Canton kept the Bridge in Amroth parish from 1822 to 1828.

David Phelps was living at Wiseman's Bridge from 1841 to 1851, and although his main occupation was farming he must have acted as innkeeper as well. The redoubtable Bridget Hodge from Pendine held the licence from the 1850s to the 1880s and she too farmed the patch of land which went with the pub. Widowed twice by the age of 34, she married for a third time in 1839 at the age of 38 and farmed near Red Roses before moving with her extended family to Wiseman's Bridge. On her death in 1888, her granddaughter Sarah (Sally) James became the new licensee, running the pub with her younger brother Ben for the next 40 years. Ben and Sally were a remarkable pair of characters about whom many stories are told. According to Mr. Roscoe Howells in his unpublished history of the inn (available at the Pembrokeshire Records Office):

> Ben had his observations to make on the farming scene. One of his remembered pearls of wisdom was on the porcine species. 'If ever thou shouldst see a old sow on the road', he would say, 'go thee up to her and give her a flyin' kick in th'arse, for thou canst venture to reckon if she isn't coming from trouble, she's gwain to it!'

Mr. Howells goes on to provide a fine description of what must have been a fairly typical Pembrokeshire country inn at the turn of the 20th century:

> Even though times were for the most part hard, there was a typical gathering of some of the local workmen on pay night. Some would manage a pint, some would settle for a sleever which was a measure of somewhere between a half and a pint. A pint was threepence at the time and a sleever twopence — sometimes it would be called for as 'a tuppenny'.

Whatever drink had been called, it would seem to have lasted through the evening, much of which would be occupied in everyone being called on in turn to do their party piece. Gramfer Ben Howells' was 'A Fox Looked Out One Cloudy Night' — all seven verses and the chorus each time. Will Prout's piece was 'Dance, Thompson, Dance' and Harry Morgan of Pleasant Green would weigh in with 'Pull for the Shore, Sailor, Pull for the Shore'. Then the assembled company would say: 'Now then Sally, thy turn next'. And Sally, with grey stockings, white garters and black boots would come forward and, in a squeaky voice, sing: 'Has Anybody seen my Yow an' Lamb'?

The last turn would be Ben, who had up to then been stretched out on the skew in his stocking feet with his toes turned out, and pretty black at that. Ben's solo was: 'Do your best for one another, makin' life a pleasant dream. Help a poor old weary brother, pullin' hard against the stream'.

Ben and Sally continued to live at the Wiseman's Bridge inn until their retirement in 1931, after which the inn was advertised as being to let together with 30 acres of land. Mr. John Mathias was the new tenant and he made a number of much-needed alterations to the premises in 1934. 'Jack the Bridge' and his wife Artie were still there when the inn received a distiguished wartime visitor in the person of Winston Churchill, who was in the area to inspect one of the logistical exercises held on the nearby beaches to test equipment and techniques prior to the Allied invasion of Normandy. Jack and Artie provided the great man with tea, sandwiches and Welsh cakes, and later received a letter from Downing Street thanking them for their hospitality.

Ben James and his sister Sally outside the Wiseman's Bridge Inn.

Picture courtesy of Mr. Roscoe Howells.

In 1947 the pub was bought by a concern called 'Wiseman's Bridge Ltd.' and more alterations and extensions were made which enabled new licensee Stanley Hunt to serve evening meals to the growing number of holidaymakers arriving in west Wales. Many of these visitors were servicemen who had been stationed in the area during the war and who were keen to return with their familes to discover the delights of Pembrokeshire in peacetime.

Typical 1960s alterations to the Wiseman's Bridge Inn completely altered the look of the building.

Ben and Sally would not have recognised the place! The new bar at the Wiseman's Bridge Inn in the 1960s.

Both pictures courtesy of Mr. Gary Davies.

In the early 1950s the Wiseman's Bridge Inn was purchased by Mr. Percy Kemble who continued the process of upgrading and extending the pub, which was subsequently run by his son, also called Percy, and Margaret Kemble. The premises were partially destroyed in a fire on Christmas Eve, 2002 which broke out in a central heating boiler. Firemen spent seven hours bringing the blaze under control and fortunately managed to save the oldest part of the inn. Now completely repaired, the pub is being run by the third generation of the Kemble family, Robert Kemble and his sisters Helen and Jane.

A view of the Wiseman's Bridge Inn today, with the fire damage completely repaired and the 1960s extension replaced by a rather more harmonious pitched-roof construction.

CHAPTER SIX

Tavernspite to Cross Hands

The origin of the name 'Tavernspite' has divided historians over the years, with some asserting that it derives from a medieval hospice which may once have stood here. However, B.G. Charles in *The Place-names of Pembrokeshire* has argued persuasively that the name came from an 18th-century inn. 'This tafarn or inn was so-called because it was opened in spite and in opposition to another tavern', he wrote. 'Sbeit, usually written Spite on maps, is not uncommon in Wales as the name of an abode which has been set up in contentious circumstances such as a dispute about the owner-ship of land'.

This remote spot on the border between Pembrokeshire and Carmarthenshire was provided with an inn because it was on the main over-land route from St. Clears westwards — part of the 'great road' from Gloucester through Brecon and Carmarthen to the ports and harbours of Pembrokeshire. This ancient roadway grew in importance in the 18th century when the packet boat service to Ireland was established at Hakin Point in Hubberston and the mail coaches began to pass this way each day. Having managed the stiff climb out of Llanddowror, the coaches would find themselves on fairly level ground all the way to Cold Blow — although the high, moorland road could be lonely and bleak and the surface was often rutted and full of potholes.

To reflect this steady increase in traffic, an inn was built at a deserted crossroads where the coach road was intersected by lanes from Ludchurch, Whitland and Crunwere. In its early days this inn must have been a less than prepossessing place — one traveller in 1775 called it a 'wretched hovel'. This original inn — which may have been the 'tavern built out of spite' — was in Carmarthenshire, on the site of what was to become the substantial **Plume of Feathers** coaching inn (now closed), described by one traveller as 'a great, gaunt, grey barrack-like building'. Tradition has it that Nelson and Lady Hamilton once called at the 'Plume', while the inn

The historic Plume of Feathers closed in the 1930s.
It was originally a three-storey building.

was caught up in the Rebecca Riots of the 1840s. However, the Plume of Feathers is technically outside the remit of this book, having been built 50 yards the 'wrong' side of the county border.

But the 'Plume' wasn't the only pub on the old crossroads. There was another 18th-century hostelry just this side of the border which also has some claims to being the source of the village name — the **Old Tavernspite**. A traveller who passed this way in 1796 described the Plume of Feathers as a 'decent inn', while the Old Tavernspite he dismissed as 'a miserable public house'. John Holland was the landlord in 1810, but following his death the following year it was run by his widow Dorothy. She subsequently married Edward Page who took over the licence and remained in charge until 1822. Isaac Phillips then ran the Old Tavernspite for a couple of years before leaving to open another pub nearby and the licensee in 1825 was Elizabeth Morris.

She appears to have changed the name of the pub to **Coach and Horses** before handing over to Philip Evans, while Henry Thomas took over the reins in 1828. (The records are scant, however, and it is possible that the Coach and Horses was in a different building altogether, and that when the Old Tavernspite closed the licence was transferred to the new premises). John Richards ran the Coach and Horses in 1841, but the pub evidently closed soon afterwards. The Rev. M.G.R. Morris, an authority on the history of Tavernspite, has stated that the Coach and Horses was on the site of what is now Myrtle Villa.

The pub which Isaac Phillips opened in 1825 was the **Union Flag** (sometimes **Union Jack**) and he was still there in 1828. The site of this pub is uncertain, but it may have become the **Ordnance Arms** which was mentioned in the *Welshman* newspaper in 1833 as a popular place for farmers and drovers to meet before and after Narberth fair. Walter Phillips was the landlord in 1841.

The 1851 census shows William Williams running a pub in Tavernspite called 'Cannons' — surely a local nickname for the Ordnance Arms, which may even have had a cannon on its sign. The mail coaches were no longer passing through the village at this time, but Tavernspite continued to grow and by 1847 it was staging its own monthly fairs. 'Tavernspite possesses

A recent view of the Alpha in Tavernspite.

every convenience for holding fairs, having excellent capacious cattle stands and being well-furnished with pens for sheep', reported one newspaper at the time. This may have prompted William Williams to change the pub name again, this time to the **Farmers' Arms,** where he remained the landlord until about 1872. The landlord from 1873 to 1887 was his son John Williams, a tailor by trade, but the pub must have closed some time around

1890. The Farmers' Arms is thought to have stood on the site of the present Burlington House.

The Plume of Feathers finally closed in 1922 — a victim of the redundancy ruling. Licensee at the time was George Williams who also farmed 40 acres of land, and the remoteness of the inn had earned it a reputation for being an 'after hours' establishment much frequented by young farm labourers. No doubt Whitland magistrates bore this in mind when, after receiving signed petitions both for and against the abolition of the licence, they decided to refer the Plume to the compensation committee.

Tavernspite was then without a pub for nearly half a century before the **Alpha** was opened in 1963 by Mr. David Higgon. Formerly a village shop and bakery, the Alpha was well-placed to take advantage of the Sunday licensing laws when Pembrokeshire voted to become 'wet' in 1968. Being just a few yards inside the Pembrokeshire boundary, the Alpha became a popular Sunday drinking destination for people in neighbouring Carmarthenshire where the pubs stayed firmly shut on the Sabbath. Mrs. Stella Higgon took over the licence in 1965 and ran the pub with the help of son Ian until 1977 when Carol James became the new licensee. The Alpha was closed for a few years in the 1990s but was reopened by Noel Corrigan, formerly of the Parcylan in Llanddewi Velfrey, and it has been run for the past five years by Louise George.

When historian Richard Fenton followed 'the great turnpike road' from Cold Blow to Tavernspite in 1810, he wrote that he seemed to remember an inn 'near Princes Gate with the sign of **Noah's Ark**'. Fenton's memory did not fail him, because the Noah's Ark was briefly a coaching inn of some importance. *Bonner and Middleton's Bristol Journal* of October 13, 1787 carried an advertisement which stated that a mail coach, operated by government authority and with a guard, would be leaving the Rummer Tavern in Bristol on a daily basis, travelling 'in a most safe and speedy manner' to the Angel Inn at Cardiff and on to Swansea. Three times a week it would continue through Carmarthen and Narberth to Haverfordwest and finally link up with the Waterford packet service at Hakin Point.

One of the places to be called at en route was the Noah's Ark at 'Brangwithnoar' where the landlord's name was Palmer, and an indication of the importance of the inn is that it was the only one named between the Red Lion in Carmarthen and the Waterford Pacquet in Hakin. It seems to have been closed for some years when Fenton passed this way, but the Rev. M.G.R. Morris in his booklet *Princes Gate* records that the inn was briefly reopened in the 1830s by two men named Davies and Fussell. It was a sadly misguided move, since the passing trade was about to be removed to the new mail coach road to Hobbs Point. John Fussell fell heavily into debt and was eventually sent to jail owing nearly £40; among his unpaid bills was one for stout from Bath and another for strong whisky and London Gin from Lewis and Thomas of Carmarthen. He had also failed to pay for a dozen rush-bottom chairs and an oak table — evidently the furnishings of the inn. It must have closed for good in the late 1830s and is now known as Blaengwaith-Noah. The name 'Noah's Ark' seems to have been a play on the Welsh name of the property which translates as — 'the start of the Gwyddno stream' — although others have have translated it as Noe's Fort — Noe being a son of King Arthur.

To the north of the 'great turnpike road' is Lampeter Velfrey, an ancient settlement on the southern edge of the fertile Lampeter Vale. The village is in an area of rich farmland, but it also has an industrial heritage, having been a long-standing centre of limestone-quarrying and lime-burning. Milling was also important here, with the streams that flow into the vale being harnessed to grind corn and also to power the machinery at the woollen factory at nearby Llanmill.

The excellent *Landsker Borderlands* leaflet on the history of the village reveals that that there was a pub in the parish in 1660. In that year Phillipp William was accused of being unfit to run an ale-house because he kept food for neither man nor beast on the premises — and even if he had, there was no Mrs. William to serve the guests as custom demanded. A hundred years later, according to the same leaflet, there was a cottage ale-house called the **Three Tuns** at the upper end of the village.

William Thomas ran an ale-house in the village from 1810 to about 1818. This was probably the **Horse and Jockey** which later closed, only to reopen briefly as the **Lime Kiln** where the licensee in 1841 was Anne Scourfield. Another short-lived ale-house about which little is known was the **Cross Inn** run by collier Edward Hodge in 1851.

The former Bush at Lampeter Velfrey still looks every inch the old village inn.

Coachman Dan Harries and his wife

Hannah were running the **Bush** in the centre of Lampeter Velfrey in 1841, and by 1847 they were hosting meetings of the Cynfelin Lodge of True Ivorites. The hard-working Mr. Harries, who was also a maltster, grocer and farmer, was still at the Bush in 1876 when the licence was transferred from one house in the village to another one adjoining, the new pub having nine rooms and a passageway through the building to stables at the back. The move didn't suit Mr. Harries who died the following year, although his widow Hannah carried on pouring the pints for a couple more years.

Martha Salmon, a widow from Nevern, took over the running of the pub in 1880 and she was still there in 1902, while James Picton was landlord from 1906 to 1908 and Mrs. Eliza Picton ran the pub between 1909 and 1933. The Bush was put up for auction after her day but struggled to attract a worthwhile bid and soon became a target for closure under the redundancy scheme. It limped along for a couple of years under licensee Eli Glover before being put out of its misery by the magistrates in April 1936. Compensation of £80 was shared between owner William Dodds of Staffordshire and licensee Mr. Glover of Brewery Street, Pembroke Dock. The building is now a private house known as Bushlands.

At nearby Llanmill is a farm called Venterin. In 1827 the local press carried adverts for the sale of **Venture In** (*sic.*), then occupied by John Griffiths. There is no suggestion that it was a pub at that time, but the name indicates that it might well have belonged to that family of early Pembrokeshire ale-houses with names like Step Aside, Step In and Stop and Call.

Surprisingly, the crossroads village of Princes Gate with its tollgate seems never to have had its own ale-house, although it did have a couple of shebeens; in 1845 Maria Lewis of Princes Gate and Sarah Beynon of nearby Redford were both fined for selling beer without a licence. Just down the road at Cold Blow, however, there was an inn of great importance in its day — the **Windsor Castle.**

The rapid rise to prominence of Tenby as a sea-bathing resort in the late 18th and early 19th centuries meant a large influx of visitors into the county. Many of these were well-to-do families who travelled in their own carriages and who took a house in the town for 'the season'. A few arrived by sea, while others took advantage of the post-chaise system, hiring chaises at the larger inns along the way. But as far as public transport went, the only overland connection Pembrokeshire had with the outside world at this time was via the mail coaches which ran to Hakin Point, and the nearest these coaches came to Tenby was when they passed along the turnpike from Tavernspite to Narberth. Aware of this problem, Sir William Paxton of Middleton Hall decided to build a new coaching inn at Cold Blow where a road forked south from the main turnpike convenient for travellers making for Tenby. Consequently, in June 1812 the following advertisement appeared in the *Carmarthen Journal:*

CAPITAL INN AND TAVERN
AT COLD BLOW
DAVID HUGHES
(Late Guard of His Majesty's Royal Mail)
Most respectfully solicits the attention of the Public to the above INN
and begs to assure those who may honor
him with their countenance and support that he has spared
neither expense nor exertion to render his House
commodious and comfortable in every department of
entertainment and accommodation; and that he has
completed his plan of accommodation by furnishing
himself with a neat POST CHAISE and Careful Drivers.

The 'Cold Blow Inn' not being the most inviting of names, it wasn't surprising that Mr. Hughes chose the grander-sounding Windsor Castle. He ran the inn for seven years and also farmed 23 acres of arable and pasture land. Hughes left at Michaelmas 1819 and the Windsor Castle was given a facelift and reopened in May 1820 by David Philipps, formerly of the Golden Lion in Narberth. He too placed an advert in the *Carmarthen Journal* informing the public that his inn was fitted out in an 'elegant and commodious manner for the accommodation of those who may honour him with their command'. The inn also boasted 'well-aired beds, good wines and foreign spirits'.

In December 1823 another advert appeared in the *Journal* offering the lease of 'that well-established inn and posting house called **Cold Blow**, situate at the entrance to the turn-pike road leading from Carmarthen' — which would suggest that the name 'Windsor Castle' never really caught on.

The Windsor Castle at Cold Blow has been a private house for 150 years.

The new licensee was William Small who took over the lease of the inn and the postal service which went with it, the landlord being responsible for the delivery of the post bags to Tenby and Pembroke. It must have been a lively place in its day, with the *Regulator* and *Telegraph* coaches calling every day on the Milford Haven run, as well as a steady stream of coaches, post-chaises and private carriages bound for Tenby. The inn possessed stabling for 15 horses and standing for five carriages.

Mr. Small met a tragic end in 1825 when he was thrown from his horse and killed instantly; his widow Mary took over the running of the inn. The Rev. Joseph Romilly who passed this way in 1827 thought Cold Blow a miserable spot — 'a single public house' — showing that the village had yet to grow up around the inn. (When it did, it wasn't much of a place; as a later visitor declared: 'The population of Cold Blow are black in the face, down at the heel and ragged of coat. The women are slatterns, the men loungers and most of them — like colliers everywhere — have a dog').

The Windsor Castle's hey-day was short-lived, as it too fell victim to Telford's new road from Red Roses to Hobbs Point. Mary Small gave up the business in March 1837, holding an auction of fixtures and fittings which lasted two days. She retired to a cottage next to the inn, and in April 1842 an advert appeared in the *Welshman* offering for sale 'All that inn, garden and premises formerly called the Windsor Castle Hotel'. The advert suggested that the property was well suited 'for being converted into an excellent premises for maltsters'. Still standing, it has been a private house for many years.

The closure of the Windsor Castle seems to have left a niche in the market which was filled by George Edwards who ran the **New Inn** between 1841 and 1851. This was located just outside Cold Blow on the road to Princes Gate, between Greenwood Farm and the present railway bridge.

The large village of Templeton is a fine example of medieval planning, with a long single main street fronted by small farms and houses, with burgage plots extending behind. The name is thought to derive from the Order of Templars which may have had a religious house in the vicinity, and the village's position on an important crossroads on the busy north-south trading link between Tenby and Cardigan ensured its continued prosperity. There was rich grazing for cattle in the pastures which surrounded the village and Templeton fair, held each November, would attract plenty of farmers and dealers to view the cattle lining the village street.

Naturally, such a thriving place had its quota of pubs — more than its quota according to the temperance movement which was active in the village. (At a Band of Hope tea-party in September 1879 the song *Do not Marry a Man if he Drinks* was 'admirably rendered by Mr. Daniel Davies').

A typical Pembrokeshire farmhouse pub, the Rising Sun in Templeton, closed 70 years ago.

One of the oldest ale-houses was the **Rising Sun** on the west side of the village street, a farmhouse pub often referred to as the 'Sun'. David Lewis was the landlord from 1795 to 1824 followed by Thomas Lewis who took over in 1825 and ran the pub for some ten years before being succeeded by his widow Frances. In April 1843 the inn was packed for the inquest on John Mabe, a local butcher who drowned in the Cleddau at Canaston Bridge while attempting to escape the custody of three Narberth constables who were transporting him to Haverfordwest gaol for the non-payment of £8 18s. licence duty. Despite hearing suggestions of what might now be termed 'police brutality', the inquest jury at the Sun returned a verdict of 'accidental death while absconding from custody'.

By 1850 Frances Lewis had taken a back seat and for the next half century the pub and 30-acre farm were run by her son Thomas and his wife Hester. They were tenant farmers, and rather surprisingly their landlord in the 1890s was the Bishop of Llandaff. This was the Rt. Rev. Richard Lewis, a member of the landowning Lewis family of Henllan near Llanddewi Velfrey, who had inherited the property. Thomas Lewis was 85 when he finally gave up the licence in 1903 and it was his granddaughter, Mrs. Selina Rees, who carried on running the pub and farm until her death in 1933. Gilbert Rees took over, but the Rising Sun was forced to close in 1934 on redundancy grounds. Compensation for the closure was set at £130.

The landlord of the **Lime Kiln** inn at Templeton from 1795 to 1822 was Thomas Bowen and from 1823 to 1826 it was John Morgan. The pub seems then to have become the **Poyer's Arms**, because that is where John

*Landlord George Morgan and family outside the Poyer's Arms
in the early part of the 20th century.*

Picture courtesy of Mrs. Betty James, Lamphey.

Morgan was licensee from 1827 until about 1850. Like the Rising Sun, this was also a farm and it was one of the oldest buildings in the village. By the 1850s, John Morgan's son Lewis Morgan was running the farm and pub and he was fined £5 for selling beer out of hours in 1863 — the severity of the fine indicating that this was unlikely to have been his first offence. No doubt the building of the railway almost alongside the pub meant some wild nights as the navvies slaked their mighty thirsts, and 'in consequence of this house not having been conducted in a satisfactory manner', the Poyer's Arms lost its licence in 1865.

It seems to have carried on as a beer-house, and after Lewis Morgan died in 1866 his widow Eliza ran the business. She remarried, and her husband William Lloyd was the landlord between 1874 and 1884. By this time the pub had a full licence again and the True Briton Friendly Society used the Poyer's Arms as its registered office in the 1880s. George Morgan — son of Eliza and Lewis — was the landlord between 1891 and 1918 followed by Elizabeth Morgan and then Edgar Morgan, a farmer and butcher, who was there between 1923 and 1933. The pub was forced to close in April of that year when the local magistrates refused to renew the licence; compensation of £120 was paid out under the redundancy ruling. The Morgans were unlucky; the police admitted that the Poyer's Arms was 'properly carried on', but they felt that three pubs were too many for such a small village, and that as the Poyer's was the one in the middle it should

The building which housed the Poyer's Arms in Templeton has been thoroughly restored.

be the one to go. It was the property of Sir Wilfred Lewis of Henllan at the time and contained two large rooms on the ground floor for business and five substantial bedrooms. The Poyer's Arms remained a sad ruin for many years until recently renovated as part of a housing association development.

Built in 1831 as an estate pub for the de Rutzen family of Slebech House, the wooden-beamed **Boar's Head** takes its sign from the coat of arms of the de Rutzens. A widow named Priscilla Williams ran the pub from 1841 to 1851, eventually handing over to her son-in-law and daughter, Priscilla and Stephen Davies. When Stephen Davies died at an early age, Priscilla married James Jones who was the landlord in 1858. Tragically, Mr. Jones also met an untimely end, dying in 1861 at the age of 39 after falling from a cart; the inquest was held in his own pub. This left the unfortunate Priscilla to bring up a large brood of children by her two marriages, which she succeeded in doing, running the Boar's Head for the next 20 years and farming 100 acres of land with the help of her son Tom.

The Boar's Head at Templeton with its distinctive half-timbered frontage.

In 1884 the landlord was John Eynon and Benjamin Owen was licensee in the 1890s. Fred Lewis was there from 1899 to 1903, followed by John John and then the long-serving Howard Davies who ran the pub from 1910 until his death in April 1953. John Kelly took over, and ran the pub for ten years, followed by Joseph and Elizabeth Jenkins in the 1960s and Irmgard Franziska Martha Binbasilar in the 1970s. The Boar's Head was once a typical two-room farmhouse pub, with a bar on one side of the front door and a sitting room on the other side where the agent of the Slebech estate would collect the rents from the tenantry on quarter days. It has been extended over the years with the addition of a restaurant and kitchen, and Derek Ashford catered for a growing number of tourists during the 1980s and '90s. For the past five years the pub has been run by local cricket umpire 'Geordie' Fraser, formerly mine host at the Parcylan Inn, Llanddewi Velfrey.

For some reason, two ale-houses opened in Templeton in 1826, neither of which lasted very long. The **Bridge End** was launched by William Davids, while local butcher Thomas Mabe also opened a pub in the village. There is no record of the name of Mr. Mabe's ale-house, and both pubs closed within 12 months.

Between Templeton and Cross Hands is an ancient property known as Peter's Finger, referred to as 'St. Peter's Finger' in Henllan estate papers for 1745. This may once have been a pilgrims' inn, since before the Reformation, St. Peter was quite a common figure on pub signs, usually being depicted holding up his hand with index finger raised to bestow a blessing. After the Reformation, the 'papist' image of St. Peter was usually replaced on ale-house signs by his symbol of the cross keys. However, there were several instances where the landlord simply sawed through the signboard to remove St. Peter, leaving the saint's hand with upraised finger as the improvised pub sign. The house would become known as **Peter's Finger** (examples have been recorded in Wiltshire and Dorset) and this may well be the case with the building near Templeton.

Tradition has it that the cottage pub which stood for many years on a crossroads between Carew and Canaston Bridge was once known as 'The Toad's Groan'. Where the name came from and what it referred to isn't known, but in the days before the Cleddau Bridge was built the **Cross Hands** inn was a regular meeting place for people travelling between the north of the county and the south. Cricketers and rugby players returning from the Saturday match would call at the inn to exchange news and scores, while shepherds moving their flocks between the Preselis and the Castlemartin Range were regular visitors.

The pub is mentioned in the 1841 census when it appears as the Cross Inn run by John Morgan; it was owned by the Slebech estate, and may have been opened at the instigation of the Baron de Rutzen. The name 'Cross Hands' first appears in 1861, when the landlord was John Thomas who lived there with his wife, daughter and niece, all of them called Elizabeth.

*The Cross Hands Inn was a popular meeting place in
the centre of the county.*

The innkeeper from 1871 to 1884 was a local blacksmith called Charles Merriman and he was succeeded by his widow Mary who was still running the pub in 1902, aged 82. By 1903 the landlord was her son Joseph Merriman and the pub was frequently 'the luncheon resort of shooting parties' which shot over the Slebech estate. Joseph had begun his career in the offices of James Williams in Narberth and worked for a time in London, Manchester and Liverpool before returning to run the Cross Hands inn and farm the land that went with it.

By this time the motoring age had arrived and the inn was well established as a stopping-off point for charabanc parties bound for Tenby from Haverfordwest. A newspaper report of 1910 disclosed that Mary Merriman was still living at the pub aged 90. The old lady, reported the newspaper, 'has a most interesting repertoire of stories relating to the period when stagecoaches held sway on the road' — although, sadly, it neglected to record any of these stories.

From 1917 to 1925 James Watkins — formerly of the Stanley Arms — was the landlord cum farmer, but in April 1925 the tenancy passed to his brother Alfred Sidney Watkins. It was still owned by the Slebech estate, and in 1935 John Frederick de Rutzen arranged for the tiny thatched pub to be enlarged by the building of a new room. The fact that he did this without first obtaining planning permission led to his knuckles being rapped by the local bureaucrats.

71

In February 1949, Alfred Watkins stepped aside to allow his son-in-law Bill Parry — a former Sergeant Major in the Royal Welch Fusiliers — to take over. Travellers and locals made the Cross Hands a busy pub at this time, and one of his first moves was to purchase a redundant 'prefab' which he installed at the back of the pub and kitted out with old bus seats to create a basic, but

The gazelle peers down from above the bar of the Cross Hands Inn.

highly popular lounge bar. Bill Parry also hung the head of a gazelle — stuffed and mounted — above the bar. This was a trophy of his war service in India and later became the focus of the Gazelle Cup, a darts tournament which raised considerable sums for charity. The gazelle head was later transferred to the Cresselly Arms, which has been run for many years by Bill Parry's daughter, Janet Cole, and her husband, Maurice.

Stewart Parry succeeded his father in 1968, but in 1973 no application was made for the renewal of the licence. Instead the site was acquired by a local builder who pulled down the characterful old inn and replaced it with a large and glitzy pub cum dance-hall set back from the road. This proved a short-lived enterprise, and the building now houses a ten-pin bowling centre.

CHAPTER SEVEN

Milton, Carew, Sageston and Jeffreyston

There is a low wall in the village of Milton which nowadays seems to serve no useful purpose. However (so the story goes) in the days when the village boasted two neighbouring pubs, the wall — which was then much higher — was built by the landlord of the **Three Horseshoes** in order to stop the rival establishment being seen by approaching customers. Blacksmith William Rees was the landlord of the Three Horseshoes in 1822 and with his wife Mary he ran the inn for many years. It was a substantial property, with a cobbled stable yard and coach-house as well as the smithy. William died in the 1860s, but Mary carried on until her death at the age of 79 in 1865. Their son-in-law Thomas Brown inherited the pub and ran it for a dozen years, while — rather unusually — the licensee in 1881 was a Hampshire man named Charles Smith. The pub closed in the 1880s, so perhaps the locals didn't take too readily to this early 'incomer'!

The former Three Horseshoes in Milton, showing the wall which the landlord built to hide the Milton Brewery inn from approaching customers.

The streams that rise on the Ridgeway and flow into the Carew River were harnessed to power the corn mill and carding mills which gave the village its name. Among the local millers were members of the Allen family, and they also turned their hand to malting barley and brewing beer at a property alongside the village stream. This development is thought to date from about 1831 when Thomas Allen built a couple of cottages on the site, while Pearce Allen was operating a malt-house there in 1841. By 1861, Florence Allen was describing herself as 'maltster and brewer' of the Milton brewery, and there must have been a tap-house attached to the brewery at this stage because the census reveals that her employees included Jane Williams, a 12-year-old barmaid. An early map shows that this brewery tap was originally called the **Bridge End**, but the name doesn't seem to have caught on and instead it became the **Milton Brewery** inn.

By the 1870s, Thomas Griffiths had become the maltster, brewer and licensed victualler, and he expanded the business by manufacturing and selling his own brand of aerated waters. This business was carried on by his widow Eliza in 1891 and subsequently by her second husband John Jones. By 1901 Mrs. Jones was a widow for the second time, but she continued to run the Milton Brewery until 1906. It is believed that brewing ceased at Milton Brewery in 1910, since when it has been run as an out-and-out pub. Con Galvin was licensee in 1912, Alfred James kept the pub from 1923 to 1930 and from the early 1930s until his retirement in 1953 the licensee was Mr. Billy Hall. He was followed by Harold Poate, formerly of Cosheston Brewery, and it was during his time that a caravan site was established on land attached to the rear of the pub. Mr. Poate left Milton Brewery in 1964, since when the pub has continued to expand from the original tap-room into an attractive and

The Milton Brewery inn as it looked in the 1960s.

74

A recent view of the Milton Brewery inn.

substantial inn, with a function room added in the old brewery building at the rear. Underneath the pool table is a well — now covered over — which must have provided the brewery with its supply of fresh water. Recent landlords have included Desmond Joyce, Tom Pritchard, Mike Griffin and Edward Mason, while the present licensee is Mr. Keith Bailey.

Sageston village, a mile or so to the east, was known in Victorian times as a centre of malting, and the malt houses and barns used by the Codd family can still be seen. There must have been an ale-house on the site at some stage, because Thomas Codd held an ale-house licence in the early 19th century, but in later years the family concentrated on farming and malting. The **Plough** on the other side of the road is a one-time cottage pub, much altered and extended over the years. In 1851 agricultural labourer John Morris and his wife Martha were living in Sageston, and it seems that they opened the pub, giving it a suitably agricultural sign. Following her husband's death, Mrs. Morris became landlady and she ran the Plough until the early 1880s, followed by her daughter Miss Elizabeth Morris who was still there in 1906. In her day the Plough was in the middle of a row of cottages, and horses and ponies which needed to be tethered in the yard at the back would have to be led through the front door of the pub and along the passageway.

From 1908 the landlord was retired local carpenter and wheelwright George Scourfield who built the mill-wheel which can still be seen in

*A group of airmen pose for a photograph outside
the Plough in Sageston in 1944.*

Picture courtesy of Mr. Deric Brock.

Carew's tidal mill, while Mrs. Elizabeth Davies was landlady in 1914. The following year the Plough — together with other properties and a great swathe of land alongside the village — was acquired by the Admiralty for the construction of a war-time airship station complete with huge hangars. Fortunately the pub survived this dramatic development and was eventually sold off by the Admiralty in 1923, together with six acres of land. Mr. E. Evans appears to have bought the pub and subsequently enlarged it, while other licensees in the 1920s were Mr. F. Lloyd and Edward J. Gibby. Daisy Young was there from 1932 to 1937 and Mr. and Mrs. Tudor Griffiths were the licensees between 1938 and 1949. During their time the air-field was once again pressed into war-time military action and the Plough became a popular social centre for off-duty air crews. (And on-duty as well. Two of the airfield runways terminated close to the back garden of the pub, and it is said that air crews would sometimes taxi to the end of the runway ready for take-off, only to leave the aircraft idling for a few minutes while they nipped over the hedge and into the Plough for a spot of 'Dutch courage' before setting off on patrol duty over the Irish Sea).

Violet Westlake took over in 1949, while Mrs. Mary Bloomfield bought the Plough in 1953. Like so many other Pembrokeshire pubs, the Plough was greatly altered and extended in the 1960s to provide meals and otherwise

*An advert for the Plough
(with its Toby Bar) in about 1970.*

cater for the tourist trade, and an advert declared: 'On most weekends customers can enjoy a homely get-together in one of the lounge bars where music for singing or listening is provided'. Mr. and Mrs. Jim Newman were the ones who renovated the Plough and they continued to run the pub in the 1970s; subsequent licensees have included Mr. and Mrs. Ken Woolgar and Mr. and Mrs. David Lee. The Plough was closed for a lengthy period a couple of years ago and there were fears for its future, but happily it is enjoying a new lease of life under present licensees Clive and Pauline Baker.

There seems to have been an ale-house at Flemington Mill, just south of Sageston, a couple of centuries ago. Thomas Rogers was the miller, and he also held an ale-house licence in 1795.

*This 2002 photograph shows how much the Plough in Sageston
has been extended over the years.*

A pub was not needed when Carew Castle was the centre of the area.

The village of Carew is steeped in history, and can boast one of the finest castles in the country, a thousand-year-old Celtic cross, a beautifully-restored tidal mill and a 14th-century church. The village has also had its share of pubs. In 1617, a chap called Sir Giles Mompesson was granted a patent which gave him the authority to licence inns throughout Britain — an inn, as opposed to an alehouse, being somewhere that provided accommodation as well as beer. Unfortunately Sir Giles so abused his position that after only four years the patent was revoked. There was still time for his agents to visit Pembrokeshire on at least two occasions, because his surviving account books for 1617 and 1620 contain three entries for the county, one of these inns being the **King's Arms** in the parish of Carew. Where this was, no-one knows.

One evening in 1803, a weary chap by the name of J.T. Barber arrived at Carew while engaged on a tour of South Wales. He spent the night at one of the two inns in the village — the first and last time that he stayed at a village pub. He was appalled to find that the main room of the inn 'served not only for parlour and kitchen and hall, but likewise for bed-room'. As he wrote in his journal:

> Everything was in unison, the discoloured state of the walls and furniture; the care-worn looks of our host and hostess; our scanty fare consisting of hard barley bread and salt butter, with nauseating ale that even our keen appetites rejected; all betokened poverty and wretchedness.

Barber and his travelling companion were eventually shown to their bedroom, which they were obliged to share with two of the landlord's children.

It was a recess built in an adjoining room and furnished with a bag of straw which was kept in place by a couple of boards crossing the niche. Vexed with accumulating plagues, we threw ourselves half undressed on the bed, but our evil destiny had yet more troubles in store. The sheets were wringing wet, so that we had reason to expect that on the morrow we should be laid up with colds and fevers. But this apprehension was soon superseded, for a legion of fleas attacked us at all points with such persevering ferocity that we were kept in motion the whole night. A number of rats also, by gamboling among our straw, held us in the fidgets, and thus the danger of obstructed circulation was avoided.

There was more ...

We had just left off cursing rustic accommodation and the itch for travelling which had led us to these sufferings, when the door opened. No light appeared, but the sound of footsteps, softly treading, passed near us. Suspecting foul play, we instantly sprang up and caught hold of a poor, ragged girl who acted as maid of the inn and who was going to sleep with the children in the other bed.

After his night at this 'house of mortification' Barber made it his rule always to finish his day's journey in a good-sized town. 'This kind of rural accommodation may appear very diverting in a narrative', he wrote ruefully, 'but to those accustomed to better fare it will be found a very serious evil'.

There's a good chance that this dismal hostelry was the **Castle Inn** and that the 'care-worn host' was George Allen who was the landlord from 1795

The former Castle Inn in Carew. with the castle in the background.

to 1828 as well as being parish clerk. A shoemaker named John Edwards was running the inn by 1841, catering for meetings of the Carew Castle Lodge of Odd Fellows which opened a lodge room at the inn in the 1840s.

In 1851 the pub nearly lost its licence, the magistrates hearing that a complaint had been made against Mr. Edwards, that he 'entertained disorderly company and suffered fighting between the hours of 11p.m. and 12 o'clock at night'. The pub was reprieved when the landlord produced a certificate of support signed by 30 'respectable persons'. Ten years later, in May 1861, Edwards committed suicide by hanging himself in the coach house of the inn during 'a fit of temporary insanity'. His widow Jane Edwards took over and ran the Castle until 1868 when the licence was transferred to Richard Davies from Martletwy and his wife Anne. In October 1878 the licence passed from Anne Davies to her brother Thomas Morgans. William Lloyd — a shipwright from Pembroke Dock — was landlord in 1881, while his daughters Elizabeth and Mary were running the pub by 1891. The Castle seems to have closed shortly afterwards; it was the house which still stands diagonally opposite the front door of the present Carew Inn.

The other ale-house in Carew at the time of Barber's visit was probably the **New Inn**. Hester Rowe was landlady there in 1822, but in 1823 the licence was taken over by George Allen who was described as a 'weaver' of Carew Bridge. This may have been the George Allen who was also the land-

A view of the Carew Inn in the early 1950s.

lord of the Castle Inn, although it could have been a relative. Either way he didn't run the New Inn for long because in 1824 and 1825 Thomas Griffiths was the licensee. Isaac Vaughan, a stonemason from Cosheston, took over the New Inn in 1826; he was still running it in 1828 although the 1841 census simply refers to him as a mason living at Carew Bridge, so the New Inn appears to have closed in the interim.

The **Carew Inn** is still very much with us, the estate pub of the Trollope-Bellew family being a place of great character. A local tailor by the name of James Freeman was the first landlord, obtaining a licence at Castlemartin licensing sessions in September 1868. It appears that in order for a fair-sized inn to be created, the second house along the village terrace was combined with the smaller corner property alongside. The Carew Inn soon became the meeting place for a Friendly Society called the Carew Ivorites Club, and 100 members gathered at the pub for a social event in June 1869. James Freeman's widow Martha was the landlady from 1874 to 1882, in which year she was fined one shilling for serving a jug of beer to the local toll-gate keeper at two minutes past closing time.

By 1891 the Carew Inn was being run by Benjamin Henton who advertised his willingness to supply luncheons, dinners and teas to visitors to the nearby castle; his widow Mrs. Eliza Henton ran the pub in 1901. Licensees in the early part of the 20th century included Charles Howard Davies and Neville Griffiths; William Scourfield was the landlord from 1923 to 1927 and Valentine Gibby was there from 1928 to 1932. In 1935 the *West Wales Guardian* reported:

*The Carew Inn appears to have been created out of
two adjoining properties.*

Mrs. Ella Ingham, Astridge, has taken the Carew Inn and intends to manage it herself. Mrs. Ingham is well known all over west Wales as a breeder and exhibitor of hunters. The old-world inn is being completely renovated and furnished upon up-to-date lines.

A group of drinkers outside the Carew Inn in about 1950. In the doorway is the landlord of the pub Mr. Robert Johnson, the author's father.

Despite this, Miss Ingham departed in 1936 and Henry Molyneaux took charge. He remained until 1948 when Robert and Anita Johnson (the author's parents) took over. Walter Belt was there from 1955 to 1960 followed by Wally and Margaret Bowen and then Jim and Babs Trainer who were licensees from 1974 to 1989. Until the building of a social club on the local sports field, the Carew Inn was the headquarters of the village's successful football and cricket clubs and Mr. Trainer was for many years the cricket club scorer. The Carew Inn still has strong sporting links and is also a regular live music venue. The present licensee is Mandy Hinchcliffe who took over the pub in 1991 in partnership with her late husband Rob.

Heading north out of Carew, the next pub was a long way up the road, on the hill from Bishop's Bridge to Yerbeston Mountain. This was the **Halfway**, where Leonard Watkins was landlord from 1822 to 1828. Now known as Bramble Cottage, it may have been a pub from at least 1810,

The New Inn at Yerbeston closed in 1909.

because John Roblyn was landlord of an ale-house at Yerbeston in that year. It had closed by 1841.

Further up the hill at the crossroads was the rather more substantial **New Inn** at Yerbeston Gate, where stood one of several tollgates built to catch the carters hauling lime and coal from the Cresselly area. The pub seems to have opened following the closure of the Halfway and William Phelps was the landlord from 1841 to 1851. William Price, a carpenter from Cosheston, kept the New Inn from 1871 to 1901 and also farmed 68 acres. When he died, the licence was taken over by his son, William Price (junior) who was still there when the pub closed in 1909. In recent years the building has housed a successful farm shop.

The former coal-mining village of Loveston has had a couple of pubs in its day. Evan Thomas ran an unnamed ale-house here in 1795, while in the 1840s John Morgan kept the **Cross Inn** at Loveston Cross. Across the valley at Reynalton there was an ale-house run by Isaac Hodge in 1795 while Henry James and farmer John Llewhellin were both licensed to run ale-houses in the village in 1812. Stonemason Isaac Jones was the landlord of a cottage pub in the 1830s and '40s, and naturally enough he called it the **Masons' Arms**. It appears to have been located just south of Castle Farm but had closed by the 1850s.

Jeffreyston is an ancient hilltop settlement which has grown up around the parish church — a landmark for miles around. The village lies on the Pembrokeshire coalfield, and anthracite was mined here for many centuries, originally in open cast trenches and later in 'bell pits'. This was a highly labour-intensive industry, and so populous was the area in the 1770s that John Wesley went out of his way to preach here to the mine-workers, while by 1801 Jeffreyston was the most densely populated rural parish in the county. There were five ale-houses in the parish in 1784 to cater for these thirsty labourers, the licensees being William Millar, Benjamin Fortune, William Cole, Mrs. Sinnott and John Phelps (although the latter probably ran the pub at Cresswell Quay).

In the late 18th century William Matthews, a visitor to Tenby, paid a call on Jeffreyston. The main object of his visit was to view the coal-pits, but the entry he made in his journal that night mainly concerned the inn which he encountered in the village. 'I call it an inn', he wrote, 'because on my enquiry for one I was recommended to this as a house which answered that enquiry'. Evidently there was no outward indication that it was a place of refreshment. As he noted:

> The walls were about six feet high, consequently no floor could exist above the ground. The roof was covered with thatch. There was no sign, nor sign-post. The naked rafters and the thatch, grown dark with age and smoke, proved that ceilings were non-essential.

Bravely entering the inn, Matthews found himself in a room about 20 feet long and fourteen wide. Gazing around, he observed two beds, corn bins, tables, washing tubs, water pitchers, six chairs and a cradle. Hams and flitches of bacon were suspended on hooks over the beds, while hanging on the walls were petticoats, stays, breeches and an old wig. A dead pig hung behind the door. There was bread and cheese on the tables and a few drinking mugs, while dogs and children chased one another around the room.

Matthews appears to have been dismayed by all this rather squalid clutter; he was even more surprised when he recounted his description to people elsewhere in Wales who all said that it sounded a perfectly respectable village inn. Unfortunately Matthews doesn't name the inn (how could he? —

The former Rose and Crown in Jeffreyston.

it didn't have a sign), but there's a good chance that it was the **Rose and Crown** where Mary Griffiths was the landlady from 1810 to 1841 when the census described her as a 70-year-old widow.

John Howell seems to have taken over the running of the pub in the 1840s, and he remained the licensee until 1881, supplementing his income by working in the quarries or as an agricultural labourer. Following his death, his widow Elizabeth took over as licensee. In 1891 the landlord was Rees Rees, while Annie Watkins held the licence from 1895 to 1909. The pub was nicknamed 'Nanny's House' at this time, and it is said that the trusting landlady would allow her customers to help themselves to refreshments and then 'settle up at the conclusion of the sitting'. The Rose

This private house in Jeffreyston was once the Prince of Wales.

and Crown didn't last very long following Nanny's departure. William Gunter ran it for a couple of years, as did William Hurlow, but it closed in 1912 and is now a private house.

Like the Rose and Crown, the **Prince of Wales** almost next door was owned at one time by the Lawrenny estate. It seems to have opened in the 1860s and the licensee from 1871 to 1894 was John Phillips. In 1873 he appeared in court charged with allowing four pigs to trespass on the high road. Phillips was fined one shilling for each pig, a sentence which so infuriated his wife that she had to be restrained by a burly policeman who eventually carried her out of the courtroom kicking and screaming.

John Phillips was succeeded by David Evans as the pub became part of the empire of Narberth wine merchants James Williams. However they must have considered fitting a revolving door, so quickly did their tenants come and go — ten in 14 years. John Davies held the licence in 1901, while other tenants included local blacksmith George Watkins, Ebenezer Ollin, Albert Bushell and William Hilling (the author's great grandfather, who was there in 1909). From 1915 to 1930 the licensee was Charles Melbourne Tucker. Elizabeth Jones took over and remained until 1936 in which year no application was made for the renewal of the licence. By this time the owners were Wm. Hancock and Co., Cromwell Brewery, Pembroke; it is now a private house.

An early Jeffreyston pub was the **New Inn** which was kept by Hannah Davies from 1822 to about 1830. In July 1842, Jeffreyston House and its estate were auctioned off and one of the lots comprised the New Inn which was then occupied by George Davies. He was known for keeping a 'well-conducted pub with good ale' and in the 1840s the Jeffreyston Friendly Society used the New Inn as its headquarters. George Davies was still the innkeeper in 1861 — aged 70 and with an eight-year-old son — but he was described as a retired innkeeper by 1871. It is thought that the house now known as Sunnyside was formerly the New Inn.

The closure of the New Inn seems to have prompted local grocer and farmer John Mills to open the **Commercial** somewhere in the village. He didn't bother to renew the licence in September 1879, so trade can't have been as brisk as he expected.

The only pub in the village today is the **Jeffreyston Inn**. The 'Jeff' was formerly the **Churchill Arms** — not through any connection with the great man, but because it was on the hill leading to the church. It was previously a small farm which was bought in 1970 by Mr. Willy John who turned one room into a fairly basic public bar complete with piano for singalongs. A few years later the pub was bought by Tommy and Brenda John and thoroughly altered and extended to cater for families and diners; they also renamed the pub at this time. The 'Jeff' has since changed hands a few times, with Tony and Chris Carvill, who were there in the 1980s, being the longest serving. Tony and Susan Dunn, the licensees for the past ten years, have turned part of the pub into a grocery shop, a happy throwback to the days when the village pub-cum-shop was at the centre of most Pembrokeshire communities. Through all

The Jeffreyston Inn was once the Churchill Arms.

*Multi-view cards, such as this one of the Cross Inn at Broadmoor,
were popular in the 1970s.*

the changes at the 'Jeff', one thing has remained constant — the presence of a female ghost, thought to be that of a Mrs. Herbert who lived in the building in the days when it was still a farm.

The **Cross Inn** at Broadmoor was well positioned to carry on a thriving trade, being at the heart of the local coal-field and also on a busy junction on the main mail coach route. It appears to have been opened in the 1840s by John Humphreys, but he died in 1848 and two years later his widow Jemima — described as 'innkeeper of Broadmoor' on her marriage certificate — married again. Her second husband was collier Richard Thomas and the couple continued to run the pub until the 1880s. William Hurlow was licensee in the 1890s; he described himself rather grandly as 'colliery proprietor' and it was his wife Elizabeth who was the publican. Richard Thomas Hurlow ran the Cross Inn (somewhat negligently, according to the police) from 1901 to 1911. The licence passed to David Jones in November 1911 and he remained the landlord until 1929 when Elizabeth Jones took over. She moved to the Prince of Wales in Jeffreyston the following year and Bertie Harts was landlord from 1930 until his death in 1943; in 1937 he was reprimanded by the magistrates for selling tea, sugar, chocolate and sweets over the bar to children. Albert Hilling then ran the pub for ten years, while Henry Wood conducted affairs from 1955 to 1962. Denis King was landlord in the early 1970s followed by Ken and Sue Lewis who added a 'family room' and improved the dining facilities during their 14 years in charge. Barry and Sharon Morgan were licensees from 1990 to 1999 and when they left they

A recent view of the Cross Inn.

87

sold the Cross Inn to Felinfoel, since when it has been run by various tenants of the brewery.

The village of Cold Inn between Broadmoor and East Williamston represents something of a mystery, since there appear to be no records of the ale-house which might have given the village its name. However, the village name was in use by the 1770s and local tradition has it that the ale-house known as **Cold Inn** was close to — or even part of — the present Cold Inn farm. Perhaps it was originally known as 'Call Inn', a name akin to 'Step Inn' and 'Venture Inn' and surely more welcoming than the later sign. However, it has also been suggested that the original village name was 'Cold End' or even 'Gould End' and that there never was a Cold Inn pub at all ...

In 1613, a *post mortem* inquisition following the death of Walter Philpin of Tenby, mentioned two properties called Kitshill and **New Inne**, both at 'Williamston Elliw' — an old name for East Williamston — and the name New Inn persisted until at least 1829. However it had ceased to be an inn long before this date; perhaps Thomas Gunter, who ran a pub in Williamston Hamlet in 1795, was the last licensee. There was also a pub in the Redberth area in the early 1800s run by one Solomon Whitta, but its name is unknown.

CHAPTER EIGHT

West Williamston to Landshipping

This pleasant corner of Pembrokeshire is now a quiet rural backwater, surrounded on three sides by the Cleddau river and its tidal branches. However, it was once one of the most industrialised parts of the county, with coal mines and limestone quarries, shipyards, corn mills, lime kilns and tanyards — and, of course, plenty of ale-houses to quench the thirst of the labourers.

West Williamston typifies this changing role; nowadays it is a peaceful residential community, but there was a time when it was one of the main sources of limestone in the county. All around the village are quarry workings, most of them connected to the river by channels cut through the mudbanks. None of the quarries is still in operation, but in its hey-day the Williamston limestone industry employed hundreds of men — enough to provide custom for four or five beer-houses — and it was common practice to send a young lad to the nearest beer-house at 10am and 3pm each day, laden with brown earthenware jars for the men's ration of beer.

The most imposing of these beer-houses was the **Cardigan** which was often pressed into service for a variety of duties in connection with the limestone quarries. In 1866 an inquest was held there

The former Cardigan Inn at the heart of West Williamston.

into the death of a quarryman killed in a blasting accident, while in February of the following year the pub was used as an emergency hospital when a premature blast seriously injured two quarrymen — John Cole, the doughty leader of Pisgah chapel choir, and John Rees.

The Cardigan had been granted a pub licence in 1865 when David Rees was the landlord; three years later he was fined 2s. 6d. for allowing his ass to stray on the highway. Rees was still the licensee in 1881 while Thomas Griffiths was landlord from 1891 to 1901. Mrs. Elizabeth Davies held the licence in 1906 but it closed as a pub in February 1910 and became a shop and later a private house called The Cardington.

A rather more rough and ready place was **Upper Houses** at the top of the village. In May 1936, West Williamston was visited by *West Wales Guardian* contributor 'Wanderer' who reported on his visit in his usual entertaining style:

> West Williamston is a village of memories. On the side of a slope, on its crest and at its base small dwellings muster. Rubbing shoulders with them are tumbledown cots in a sad state of decay. Yet they are homely, these old houses. At the end of a cul-de-sac you can discover 'Upper Houses'. Why 'Upper Houses' I don't know. They really are two small cottages.
>
> Home-brewed beer was brewed in one of them and sold over the bar in the other. The five quarries were then in full swing. Williamston stone was famous. Burly men hacked it out of place or blasted it with powder. The stone was shipped in coastal vessels, and when the barges called the crews came ashore and with the quarrymen repaired to 'Upper Houses'. Then the rafters rang. Pint pots went round and the landlady — a grandmother of Mrs. Hall of Milton Brewery — was often unable to cask the beer. It was sometimes sold hot. Those were the days.

'Wanderer' added that he had spoken to 82-year-old George Scourfield who could remember 'the men who used to call and crack a joke with the genial hostess, and the chalk tallies on the wall to show how much was due for liquor on the nod'.

Down the lane beyond Upper Houses, the **Ship** at Williamston Park stood right at the heart of the network of limestone quarries and canals. It was kept by Ann Ormond from 1810 right through the 1820s, and although the 1841 census merely described her as a 75-year-old farmer, it's likely that she was still running a beer-house at the time. When it ceased to be a licensed house isn't known.

Back in the heart of the village, the **Wheatensheaf**, like the Cardigan, was handy for inquests. In 1864 it was the scene of an inquiry into the death of quarry foreman John Picton who had been killed in an accident involving a crane in the docks. Ann Henton ran the pub from 1871 to 1891 and it appears to have been located between Williamston House and the Cardigan.

According to local tradition there was also a fifth beer-house in the village called the **Lion**, and a property of that name was occupied by a seaman called Thomas Arthur at the time of the 1891 census. It stood at the Williamston end of Rosemary Lane.

Upstream of West Williamston along the Cresswell River lies Cresswell Quay, another place whose present tranquillity belies a busy industrial past. It was at Cresswell Quay that barges would be loaded with coal from the mines around Cresselly and Jeffreyston, and the remains of several stone quays can still be seen — each of the local landed estates having its own quay. Cresswell House alongside one of the quays was once the home of Hugh Wilson, coal-yard manager and land agent for the Harcourt Powell estate. Wilson held an alehouse licence from 1810 to 1827, presumably to provide home-brewed refreshment for the men who shovelled the estate-produced coal and sailed the barges — although whether it was ever an out-and-out pub is debatable.

The Cresselly estate certainly owned a pub at Cresswell Quay. This was the **Square and Compass** which was run for many years by the Phelps family and may have been the ale-house for which John Phelps of Jeffreyston parish held a licence between 1784 and 1822. Henry Phelps became the licensee of the Square and Compass in 1825 and continued running the pub and farming the land around it until at least 1861; when she was old enough, his daughter, Sarah ran a grocery shop from part of the building.

Mr. Phelps wasn't always popular with his neighbours, as the *Pembrokeshire Herald* revealed in March, 1847:

> On Wednesday night last there were a great many of the family of Rebecca assembled in the field of a publican at Cresswell Quay and in a few minutes they accomplished their designs. They first began tearing down the hedge at the publican's field and then engaged themselves in tearing down a freeth (*sic*) which had been made on the previous day. The motive the publican had in view was to stop a road which passes through his field and leads to a well that supplies the neighbourhood with water — the road has been open to the public upwards of 100 years. So far the publican has been successful.

In 1861 the daughter of the household, Sarah Phelps, married a farmer from Thorn whose name, coincidentally and confusingly, was Henry Phelps. The couple set up home in Cresswell House, the former home of Hugh Wilson, and soon afterwards took over the running of the Square and Compass. They changed the name to the **Quay Head** and upgraded it from a beer-house to a fully-licensed pub in 1872, also carrying on the grocery business. Oddly, perhaps, Henry and Sarah chose not to live on the premises, and throughout the 1870s and '80s they carried on living at Cresswell House, which is where they brewed the beer to be sold in the nearby pub. As is often the case, the new pub name didn't stick for long and by 1875 the licensing records show Henry Phelps as being in charge of the Square and Compass. He remained the licensee until at least 1891, but in 1895 Sarah Phelps was running the business on her own.

It was in the late 1890s that the local squire — Henry Seymour Allen of Cresselly House — decided that a suitable hostelry was needed on the estate where locals and hunt followers could gather, and where intrepid early tourists could be provided for. He decided to convert the Square and Compass into a comfortable inn — complete with four or five bedrooms — which he renamed the **Cresselly Arms**. The newly-refurbished inn opened in 1896 and a Cardiff newspaper carried the following account in its 'Cycling News' column in 1901:

> The little village of Cresswell Quay is an ideal centre for a week or so's stay in Pembrokeshire, standing as it does at equal distance almost from Pembroke, Pembroke Dock, Tenby, Haverfordwest, Narberth, St Florence, Manorbier Castle etc. Cresswell Quay is near the ancestral home of the Allen family and is reached by a good road from Tenby.
>
> The district is very sparsely populated and yet it boasts a modern and splendidly-furnished country inn called the Cresselly Arms. The visitors who are lucky enough to find accommodation at this hotel are allowed to wander through the beautiful woods and gardens which reach the water's edge and are the property of Mr. Seymour Allen. This gentleman, it may be remarked, recently built the hotel, feeling that such a beautiful district should provide some accommodation for those who desired to linger in the district.

Sarah Phelps retired when the Cresselly Arms opened and George Davies — formerly butler at Cresselly House — was the first licensee. He was succeeded by his widow, Sarah, in 1911 and when she died in September 1936 the licence passed to their son James Davies. 'Jim the Pub' was a keen crick-

Captain Hugh Allen outside the Cresselly Arms in the 1920s.
Picture courtesy of Mr. Robert Scourfield.

eter and played in the village side skippered by Squire Allen's nephew Captain Hugh Allen. The Cresselly Arms was a thriving establishment at this time, despite the efforts of the local Baptist Chapel at Pisgah to turn the locals away from the demon drink. In 1902, 33 people signed the pledge at a temperance meeting in the chapel schoolroom,

A meet of the hounds at the Cresselly Arms in the 1930s.
Picture courtesy of Mr. Robert Scourfield.

*Mrs. Alice Davies —
'Alice the Quay'.*

while Miss Annie Lodwick, who was minister of Pisgah in the 1920s, described herself as an 'unblushing prohibitionist'.

'Jim the Pub' remained landlord until his death in 1961 when his widow Alice took over. By this time the pub had long ceased to be run as an hotel, but Mrs. Davies continued to serve hunt and cricket followers, locals and holidaymakers in the tiny bar of the Cresselly Arms until she was well into her 90s — by which time she was reputed to be the oldest licensee in the country. When Mrs. Davies finally retired she continued to live at the Cresselly Arms where she was cared for by new licensees Maurice and Janet Cole and enjoyed welcoming a constant stream of visitors, eventually passing away at the grand old age of 105.

Mr. and Mrs. Cole have continued to run 'The Quay' as a traditional, unspoilt Pembrokeshire pub — no bar-meals, no music, beer straight from the barrel — and they were rewarded when a recently-published book voted the creeper-covered Cresselly Arms the second best pub in the whole of Britain.

Its position at the junction of the Carew and Cresswell Rivers and the Milford Haven waterway meant that Lawrenny Ferry was for many years a busy river port. Shipbuilding was carried out on the foreshore, ferries crossed from here to Rhooseferry and Cosheston, and cargoes of coal and limestone were exported to harbours along the Bristol Channel. With the decline in coastal trading, Lawrenny Ferry began to develop as a yachting and holiday centre, and now has a landing-stage, boatyard and chandlery. Lawrenny village itself, a mile away in the midst of rolling farmland, once staged regular steeple-chase meetings and the stables of local squire John Frederick Lort Phillips sent out the winner of the 1905 Grand National.

Back in the 1780s, Lawrenny would have been a good place to go on a pub crawl, since there were no fewer than seven ale-houses in the parish — most of them in the area of the quay. Sadly, the names of very few of these are recorded, one exception being the **King's Head** which was kept by John Ormond in 1784. Another early pub was the **Ship** where John Power was the landlord between 1784 and 1795, but the exact whereabouts of these two early pubs is unknown. (The other licensed ale-house keepers in the parish in 1784 were Thomas Rogers, John Hill, Esther Daniel, Elizabeth Wilson and Griffith Harries).

One pub which we do know about was the **Coach and Horses** which was beautifully situated on the shore facing Benton Castle. John Griffiths, pilot and publican, kept the Coach and Horses between 1810 and his death in 1860, by which time he was 83. According to Mason:

> Captain John Griffiths, whose daughters subsequently kept the Coach and Horses, just above Lawrenny Quay on the river-side, so well-known to all trippers of by-gone days, was a renowned harbour pilot who also traded in his own smack, and it is said that he had a raven so attached to the vessel and crew that it would follow her to Ireland and back. The picture of this grand old skipper's vessel was hung in the best room of the inn and was shown with commendable pride to visitors by the pilot's daughters.

One of these daughters was Ann Griffiths, who took over the running of the pub when her father died. Her sister Frances Griffiths was the licensee from 1873 until her death in 1879, after which the pub was closed for a few months. It was taken over by two more unmarried sisters, Frances (Fanny) Bowen, 27, and her sister Mary, 18, and it continued to be a lively place during Lawrenny horse-race meetings as well as being popular with boat-trippers from Pembroke Dock. Frances was still the publican in 1891 but the Coach and Horses closed some time before 1895. It is now a private house called 'Coaches'.

Lawrenny Ferry from the Cosheston shore. The Brig and Cutter once stood on the site of the white building on the left, while the building behind the mast of the yacht is the old ferry house which for a short time doubled as the Ferry Arms public house.

Just round the corner, facing the Cosheston shore, was the **Brig and Cutter**. Joseph Evans was the landlord from 1810 to 1828, but by the time of the 1841 census he was merely describing himself as 'mariner' (and a fairly ancient one at that). It seems that the Brig and Cutter was located in the building which was later known as Quay House and which became the Rectory in the 1850s. It is now derelict.

Two rowing boat ferries ran from Lawrenny Ferry at one time, one of them making the short hop to the Cosheston shore and the other crossing the Cleddau to land at Rhooseferry near Burton. The ferryman usually lived at Ferry House, which is still standing on the shore, and for a brief period in the 1840s and '50s this was also a pub, the **Ferry Arms**. The licensee was the ferryman Thomas Davies.

The landlady of the **Rope and Anchor** from 1795 to 1828 was Ann Wilson. She seems to have been related to Hugh Wilson of Cresswell Quay, and the census returns for 1841 and 1851 show her living in retirement at Lawrenny Ferry in a property at the eastern end of the quay. By the 1860s, the properties in this area had been redeveloped to cater for the local squire's love of hunting, with the building of kennels for a pack of foxhounds and houses for the kennelman and huntsman. One hundred years later the buildings were converted once more, this time into an attractive waterside pub called the **Kirkland Arms** and later the **Lawrenny Arms** — invariably known to locals as 'The Doghouse' in memory of its previous use. As the official name suggests, the pub was owned by the Lawrenny estate and the first person to run it was Mary Glynn, a member of the Lort Phillips family. Lawrenny Ferry was developing as a boating centre at

The Lawrenny Arms in the 1960s.

the time, known as the Lawrenny Yacht Station, and the pub doubled as the local yacht club. It was subsequently extended with the addition of an accommodation block, and after being sold by the estate was eventually bought in the late 1970s by Mr. Percy Edmunds, along with the rest of Lawrenny Yacht Station. The pub, which remains in the Edmunds family, has since been run by various managers.

Once the kennels of the local foxhounds, the Lawrenny Arms is still known to locals as 'The Doghouse'.

In the village itself stood the **New Inn** which was opened in the 1840s by tailor George Davies; by the time of the 1861 census he had become 'innkeeper and parish clerk'. He remained licensee until his death in 1874, after which William Bowen, a butcher from Garron, ran the pub until 1879 when failing health saw his daughter Frances Bowen take over. The New Inn closed the following year and the family moved to the Coach and Horses where William Bowen died soon afterwards.

Tradition has it that the New Inn was closed in summary fashion by the local squire who became angry one day when his estate workers were late returning to the fields after spending their lunch-break in the pub. This story is given credence by the following newspaper account which appeared in the autumn of 1880, written by a correspondent who had, with some difficulty, travelled to Lawrenny to report on the local steeplechase meeting:

> If ever a race meeting could win a title to the term 'select', Lawrenny might safely be backed against the field to do so. Buried in a remote, unfriendly corner of the world, it can be reached only with difficulty by non-resident lovers of the sport, and the goal finally attained, nothing but starvation

stares one in the face. The village, hundred or hamlet or whatever it may be has no inn — the only abiding refuge for one who is hungered and athirst in a strange land. The squire, when he closed the solitary public house in the village, could scarcely have given thought to the needs of those attending the race meeting ...

(On a race day two years later, Lawrenny blacksmith William Thomas did his best to remedy this lack of a licensed inn. He tried the old trick of selling a biscuit for fourpence and giving away a 'free' glass of whisky to accompany it, thinking he could escape the law that way. He couldn't, and was duly charged with selling beer and whisky without a licence.)

Further up the river is the small and scattered community of Coedcanlas, best known these days as the birthplace of the jockey and thriller writer Dick Francis. In 1750 a ferryman named Evan Davies agreed a lease with Sir Arthur Owen for the rights to the ferry crossing between Llangwm and Coedcanlas together with the ferry house and two cottages on the shore. One of the cottages seems to have been an alehouse, and in 1795 Owen Davies of Llangwm Ferry, Coedcanlas, held an alehouse licence. It seems likely that this would have been for the **Square and Compass**, although the name does not appear until later. The name suggests that this was an alehouse frequented by stonemasons as well as ferry passengers, and there were once significant lime-

The former New Inn in Lawrenny which was allegedly forced to close by the local squire.

stone quarries fronting the river here. Daniel Lewis kept the Square and Compass from 1810 until his death, aged 84, in 1835, while the 1841 census shows Ann Lewis as the innkeeper at Llangwm Ferry, Coedcanlas. No refer-ences to this cottage inn seem to exist after this date.

The **Ferryside** was also an ale-house down on the shore at Llangwm Ferry, but it did not appear until some 30 years after the Square and Compass closed. In Victorian times, a boatman and oyster-fisherman from Llangwm named William Skyrme operated the rowing boat ferry between Llangwm Ferry and Port Lion near Llangwm. He was helped in later life by his son John, and by 1871 William — then aged 70 — was running an inn at his cottage home while John was doing most of the rowing. William Skyrme still held a licence for the Ferryside in 1885, but the 1891 census makes no mention of an inn at the ferry house.

The end of coal-mining at nearby Landshipping seems to have sounded the death-knell for the little cottage alehouse known as **New Inn** which stood between Martletwy and the hamlet of Weston. It was opened in the 1840s by a widow named Elizabeth Gay, and when she died in about 1860 the beer-house died with her. It is now a private house named Fern Hill.

An ivy-covered ruin on the road from Martletwy to Cresswell Quay is all that remains of the **White Lion** which appears as 'White Lyon' on a map dated 1773. William Eynon, an agricultural labourer, was the alehouse keeper at the White Lion in the 1850s and his widow Sarah was running the pub by 1871, when she was described in the census as a 64-year-old farmer and publican. She was still running the pub in 1876, but didn't bother to renew the licence the following year. In February 1883, one of Sarah's sons — Benjamin, of the White Lion, Martletwy — appeared in court charged with 'allowing a house to be inhabited, totally unfit for habitation'. Apparently Benjamin created a great deal of amusement in court 'by the towering passion he was in'.

Although the village of Martletwy seems to have been surrounded by ale-houses, there is no record of any licensed premises in the village itself. Vague references exist to the **Royal Oak** at Martletwy but there is nothing to indicate where this was or when it was open, although it may have been run by one of the three people listed as ale-house keepers in the parish in 1795 — Catherine Davies, Richard Griffiths and Richard Barzey.

At nearby Landshipping, a rowing-boat ferry once carried passengers across the river to Picton Ferry while shipbuilding was also carried out on the shore. But by far the biggest industry was coal-mining, with the anthracite from numerous local pits being exported from Landshipping Quay. Catering for the miners and ferry passengers was the **Landshipping Inn**, a substantial property in Victorian times, which like many rural Pembrokeshire pubs doubled as a farm and later as the village shop. An inventory taken in 1857 shows that the outbuildings included a stable, brewhouse, piggery and dairy, along with 32 acres of farmland.

The Landshipping Inn was owned and built by the Owen family who were a major political force in the county and who held substantial estates throughout Pembrokeshire. Their mansion at Landshipping was one of the largest in the county, but this was abandoned in the late 18th century in favour of Landshipping 'New House' down by the river facing Picton Castle. It is said that materials from the old mansion were used to build the newer house, and perhaps some of the stone and slate also went into the building of the inn. The first recorded landlord was George Thomas Husband who ran the inn in 1835 as a tenant of the Owen family. Husband had had a long association with the

Owens; he had farmed on their land at Monkton as a young man before graduating to becoming a butler at Orielton House. As a farmer and trained servant he must have been the ideal man to run the pub, and he stayed there until 1845 when he left to run the Clarence at the top of Pembroke Street in Pembroke Dock.

In 1842 the Loyal Prince of Wales Lodge of Odd Fellows was established at the Landshipping Inn with its own lodge room, and the following year 60 members of the Friendly Society, many of them colliery workers, assembled at the inn to celebrate the first anniversary of the Lodge. Dressed in full Odd Fellows regalia they paraded to Martletwy Church for a service and then marched back to Landshipping New House where they were received by local squire Lt. Col. Hugh Owen. They then returned to the Landshipping Inn where Mr. and Mrs. Husband provided a 'sumptuous dinner'.

Among those miners who sat down to that dinner, resplendent in their Odd Fellows sashes, must have been many who perished in the horrific Garden Pit catastrophe of February 14, 1844. More than 40 men and boys were drowned when the waters of the Cleddau River poured in upon them as they mined the seams which extended far under the river. The community took a long time to recover from this disaster, and it may have had some bearing on George Husband's decision to leave Landshipping the following year to take over the Clarence. His replacement at the Landshipping Inn was Thomas Sayse from Warren. As well as keeping the inn, he was a farmer, grocer and flour dealer, boosting his business by supplying all the catering needs of the Landshipping coal industry as it slowly recovered from the 1844 disaster.

In 1857, the Owen family found itself faced with massive debts incurred in fighting elections, and Sir John Owen was forced to sell off many of his estates to pay his creditors. Most of Landshipping, including the inn, went under the hammer in April 1857, and Thomas Sayse gave up the tenancy at Michaelmas of that year. (Evidently he was well thought of by the Owens, because some years later he took over the Speculation Inn on the Orielton estate).

The purchaser of the 4,700 acre Landshipping estate was Major James Talbot Stanley of Brighton. The estate later passed to his son, James Douglas Talbot Stanley, but the Stanley family seems never to have lived in the area on a permanent basis, its members preferring to reside in Brighton or even Brussels and only making occasional visits to Pembrokeshire. By 1861 the innkeeper was a local tailor named John Merriman, but he soon returned to his old trade, giving way to Thomas Noot from across the river at Boulston. Noot farmed the land while his wife Margaret ran a grocer's shop from part of the pub; they later expanded their activities by adding a post office, while the Odd Fellows connection remained until at least 1880 when it was still the registered office of the Lodge. Thomas Noot ran the Landshipping Inn for over 40 years, becoming such a fixture in the district that the pub was invariably called 'Noot's'.

Samuel Gwyther took over the pub from the Noots in 1910 when the name was changed to the **Stanley Arms**. The licence passed to Thomas Gwyther in 1912, but James Watkins ran the pub during the First World War, followed by William Allen in 1918. The Stanley family sold the estate in 1922 when much of it was purchased by Hugh J.P. Thomas of Castle Hall, Milford Haven. The sale particulars show that the Stanley Arms then comprised 59 acres of land, a bar, two kitchens, a club-room, six bedrooms, two sitting rooms and a box room. The outbuildings included a dairy, wash-house and bake-house, a three-stall stable, a waggon-house, a cow-shed and two pig-sties. Hugh Thomas died shortly afterwards and the estate was broken up still further, with the Stanley

The Stanley Arms at Landshipping during the days of William Allen. The roof seems to show the patching-up after the fire in 1942.
Picture courtesy of the Stanley Arms.

being purchased by the tenant, William Allen. He continued to hold the licence and farm the land around until 1955.

The inn was badly damaged by a fire which broke out in May 1942. Part of the roof collapsed and several ceilings gave way before the firemen — pumping water from the river — managed to bring the blaze under control. Reported the *Tenby Observer*:

The bar at the Stanley Arms that evening presented a drippy appearance, with water streaming down from the ceiling. But customers, with remarkable dexterity, dodged in and out and business was carried on in a cheerful spirit.

William Allen was followed in the late 1950s by his son Gilbert Allen. Gilbert is remembered as being a real country character who would often abandon the pub to attend to his farming duties. Customers who wanted a drink would have to ring a bell on the bar, whereupon Gilbert would break off from his work in the farmyard and rush into the pub to pour the pints. By this time a few intrepid holidaymakers were beginning to find their way to this remote corner of Pembrokeshire, and they were often alarmed by the sight of Gilbert

The Stanley Arms as it looked in 2002.

suddenly materialising behind the bar, caked in muck and straw, asking them what they wanted to drink.

As the tourist trade increased, so the Stanley Arms has been altered and expanded to cater for their demands, particularly in the late 1960s by landlord Bernard Webber, and these days it is popular with summer visitors as well as locals.

The 'three horseshoes' sign was the heraldic device of the Worshipful Company of Farriers, and is often found on pubs where the innkeeper was also the local blacksmith. This was certainly the case with the **Three Horseshoes** at Landshipping, which was regularly described in Victorian times as 'beer-house and smithy'. In the 1840s and '50s the publican was Henry Tribe, while the blacksmith was his son-in-law James Prickett. By the

1870s another Prickett — Thomas — was acting as both blacksmith and licensed victualler, a dual role he carried on well into his 70s. When he died in 1883, his widow Bridget continued running the pub, taking in a 'boarder' named George Davies to act as the village blacksmith. By 1895 young George

The former Three Horseshoes in Landshipping.

and his wife Biddy had taken over the pub as well and he remained the licensee until 1930.

In 1931 the landlord was David Morgan Edwards, and that year saw the 'siege of the Three Horseshoes' when county court bailiffs arrived at the pub to repossess a piano. The locals duly barricaded the doors and the bailiffs were forced to leave empty handed. This didn't endear Mr. Edwards to the authorities, and when the magistrates were looking to close one of the village pubs a couple of years later on 'redundancy' grounds, it was the Three Horseshoes which had the chop. It is now a private house, aptly re-named 'The Forge'.

A mile or so out of the village is Whitlow farm where the farmer Roger Edwards held an ale-house licence in 1812. If the ale-house ever had a name it hasn't come down to us.

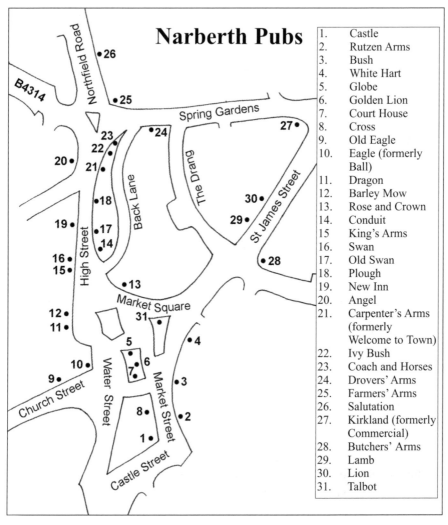

Narberth Pubs

1. Castle
2. Rutzen Arms
3. Bush
4. White Hart
5. Globe
6. Golden Lion
7. Court House
8. Cross
9. Old Eagle
10. Eagle (formerly Ball)
11. Dragon
12. Barley Mow
13. Rose and Crown
14. Conduit
15 King's Arms
16. Swan
17. Old Swan
18. Plough
19. New Inn
20. Angel
21. Carpenter's Arms (formerly Welcome to Town)
22. Ivy Bush
23. Coach and Horses
24. Drovers' Arms
25. Farmers' Arms
26. Salutation
27. Kirkland (formerly Commercial)
28. Butchers' Arms
29. Lamb
30. Lion
31. Talbot

CHAPTER NINE

Narberth
CASTLE STREET TO MARKET SQUARE

The attractive little town of Narberth has a long and colourful history, being mentioned in the collection of early Welsh folk tales known as the *Mabinogion*. Following the Norman invasion, the small settlement found itself on the uncertain frontier separating the Anglo-Norman settlements in the south of Pembrokeshire from the dispossessed Welsh in the more mountainous north. A castle was built to help keep the disgruntled natives in their place, and soon a small township grew up to the north of the castle walls.

Narberth began to blossom when it was granted permission by James II to hold a market in the town square every Thursday as well as three fairs each year, in March, May and September. Horses, cattle, pigs and sheep changed hands at these fairs, while the markets attracted vendors of grain, cheese, poultry, merchandise and fish — the latter incurring regular complaints because of the 'fearful stench' which lasted for days after each market. Country people, drovers and dealers came to the fairs and markets from miles around, and when the trading was over — and often before — they would head for the nearest ale-house to spend some of the proceeds of the day. In 1784 there were 12 people licensed to keep ale-houses in Narberth; by 1795 the figure had crept up to 13, while there were 18 pubs in the town in 1813 and an impressive total of 24 in 1826.

Many of these were simple terraced ale-houses, where horses would have to be led in through the front door and along the passage of the pub to reach the tiny stables at the back. Others would have been fully-fledged coaching inns catering for the stage coach traffic on the busy mail route from Tavernspite to Haverfordwest and Milford Haven. Chief amongst these early coaching inns were the Golden Lion and the White Hart on the Market Square, together with the rather less fashionable Rose and Crown, King's

Three (and possibly four) former Narberth hostelries can be seen in this 1907 postcard view. The Golden Lion is on the immediate left and the Globe is the building three doors further along with the lamp outside; it had become a temperance hotel by this time. Beyond the Globe can be seen the building which is thought to have housed the Old Conduit at one stage, while the Rose and Crown on the right was the only one of the four pubs still open at the time of the photograph.

Arms and Angel in High Street. Of these five historic inns, the Angel is the only survivor.

Many of the smaller ale-houses of the time are also long forgotten. The Red Cow, the Fishguard Arms, the Unicorn, the Bolt-in-Tun and the Black Horse were all thriving pubs in Narberth in the 1820s but seem to have disappeared for one reason or another during the 1830s — victims, perhaps, of the redevelopment of the town, in particular the building works carried out in Market Street. The loss of these early pubs was more than offset by the arrival of the beer-house. By the early 1850s there were 24 beer-houses in the town as well as half a dozen 'proper' inns which still served spirits, including the

Angel, the King's Arms and the Rose and Crown. The White Hart and the Golden Lion were on their last legs by this time, having been superseded by the Rutzen Arms, a purpose-built coaching inn on the grand scale, constructed in 1833 for Baron de Rutzen.

Virtually all these places brewed their own beer, and there were several maltsters in the centre of town to supply them with malted barley. In 1830, these maltsters included Arthur Williams, a brother of James Williams who founded the wine and spirit enterprise which dominated the Market Square area of Narberth for many years.

So busy did Victorian Narberth become on fair days and market days that even the great number of ale-houses struggled to cope with the crowds. This naturally led to the opening of several shebeens in the town, and in 1855 Rachel Davies, Mary Rees, Benjamin Thomas and Morris Williams were all fined for selling beer without a licence on the eve of Narberth fair. By the 1880s, Narberth's reputation as a hard-drinking town had spread beyond the boundaries of Wales. No less a publication than the *Birmingham Post* reported in 1889:

> In the little Pembrokeshire town of Narberth there are 25 public houses to a population of 1,200 — that is one public house to every 45 persons. Excluding children, this means there is at least one public house to every score of persons!

The newspaper continued: 'Out of the 25 public houses, upwards of 23 are kept — so we are told — by members and deacons of Baptist and Independent churches'. As might be expected, the article provoked considerable outrage in Narberth, particularly among the Nonconformists in the town whose temperance credentials were being called into question. A canvass of the 25 public house keepers was quickly carried out. This disclosed that, in actual fact, eight of the publicans were Baptists, five were Independents (none of them deacons) and the other 12 were church-goers. The results of this unusual poll were published in the *Pembroke and Pembroke Dock Gazette* as follows:

> Evan Phillips (Commercial Inn) Baptist;
> David Brown (Lion) Churchman;
> David Phillips (Butchers' Arms) Baptist;
> Mrs. Lilian Baker (Bush Tavern) Independent;
> W.H. Hodge (Rutzen) Churchman;
> F.L. Childs (Castle) Churchman;
> Benjamin Morris (Cross Inn) Churchman;
> Daniel Evans (Old Eagle) Baptist;
> James Bevan (Eagle) Churchman;

James Savage (Court House) Churchman;
Thomas James (Dragon) Independent;
J.R. Ormond (Rose and Crown) Churchman;
Thomas Thomas (Barley Mow) Independent;
John Davies (Conduit) Churchman;
Benjamin Howells (King's Arms) Baptist;
John Toohig (Plough) Churchman;
George Harries (Angel) Churchman;
Isaac Thomas (Carpenters' Arms) Churchman;
John Griffiths (Ivy Bush) Baptist;
Thomas Thomas (Coach and Horses) Churchman;
Thomas Williams (Drovers) Baptist;
Evan Phillips (Farmers) Independent;
John James (Salutation) Independent;
John Henton (Plaindealings) Baptist;
James Williams (Providence) Baptist.

Meanwhile, the local press was quick to respond to the 'Brummagem shot at Narberth' as it was described. The *Welshman's* correspondent took angry issue with the figures quoted in the Birmingham newspaper. 'In the whole parish, it is true, there are 25 public houses', he spluttered, 'but in the town itself there are only 23'. (Which was hardly the most convincing rebuttal to the charge that Narberth was awash with boozers).

Another correspondent took a more realistic line. 'It must be confessed', he wrote, 'that the number of public houses looks large, but we should remember that Narberth has a good weekly market and that fairs are held there once and sometimes twice a month. The town, being the centre of a large, thickly-populated and prosperous agricultural district, it follows that these markets and fairs are very largely attended and the public houses depend very largely for their support on the country people'.

Statistics tended to back the view that most drink-related problems in Narberth were caused by outsiders. Of the 33 people convicted of drunkenness in 1887, two were locals and 31 were tramps. And when, in February 1919, Police Sergeant Thomas reported a dramatic increase in the amount of drunkenness in the town, he was careful to add: 'The Bench and the public will be interested to know that 75 of those summoned were aliens from Pickle Wood'. (This didn't refer to inebriated Martians as might be supposed, but to refugees, many of them Russian Finns, working in forestry labour camps).

It was probably the pressing need for market-day accommodation which led the Redundancy and Compensation Committee to deal fairly leniently with Narberth. Only a few places came under the axe — the Court House, the Plaindealings Arms and the Plough among them — so that there still remain a couple of areas of the town with a surprisingly high concentration of pubs.

But as the market declined in importance and finally closed, and as drinking habits changed, so the number of pubs in town gradually dwindled. This trend was already apparent in 1935 when 'Narberthian' contributed an article to the *West Wales Guardian* lamenting the loss of an important social amenity. 'One cannot withhold a high degree of admiration for the successive licensees of the numerous houses once visible in this town,' he declared. 'Without the accommodation these houses provided, the gathering together of people each week could not be maintained and in a variety of other directions these old licensed victuallers of Narberth played useful parts. It must not be forgotten that at an earlier period the only social intercourse possible was provided by means of these licensed houses, and the only luxury most of the old people could afford was a couple of pints of home-brewed ale each night, with "extras" on Thursdays and Saturdays'.

Narberth itself has not always looked as bright and flourishing as it does today and few people had a good word to say about the place in the 19th century. 'The town presents a very indifferent appearance', declared one writer in 1844, while the Rev. John Morris conceded in 1897 that the place was widely referred to as 'Dirty Little Narberth'. Charles Harper, who passed this way in 1905, was even harsher, describing Narberth as 'a miserable little ash-coloured townlet' and 'the beastliest place on the whole course of the road through South Wales'.

The first inn which travellers would have encountered as they entered the town from the south would have been the **Castle Inn** which is mentioned in the *Carmarthen Journal* of August 1811. A map of the town dated 1849 shows the Castle Inn to be located in a building alongside the castle entrance, facing up Market Street, but it evidently moved at some stage because for most of its existence it was in Market Street itself, more or less opposite the Rutzen Arms.

In 1823 the Castle was kept by Thomas John, with a carpenter and cabinet maker named Lewis Watkins taking over the licence in 1824. A regular meeting place of the Ancient Briton Friendly Society, the Castle remained Lewis Watkins' preserve for well over 30 years, and he was still there in 1861. Watkins' daughter Jane was licensee in 1867, while the business had been renamed the Castle Hotel by 1869 when it was owned and run by a woolstapler named William Thomas. He departed in June 1876 to be followed by John Gay (junior), a carpenter from Martletwy.

From 1879 to 1901 the licensee and owner was Frederick Lloyd Child from Begelly. The son of 'Squire Child' of Begelly House, he was a skilled cabinet maker, a keen angler and an ardent Conservative. Mr. Child carved his own gravestone at the age of 88, just leaving a space for the date of his death to be inserted; this didn't have to be done for another eight years. Mr. Child had long retired by that time, the pub passing through several pairs of hands in the years leading up to the First World War. Fred Eynon was there the longest, from 1911 to 1914, and he was followed for five years by Elizabeth Underwood. Another rapid turnover of licensees in the early '20s prompted the local magistrates to consider closing the pub under the redundancy ruling, but it survived and George Perkins was the landlord from 1923 to 1935.

The licence then passed to Mrs. Eliza Perkins who remained a further ten years. Sidney and Queenie Bibby were in charge during the post-war years while Olive and Charlie Johnson, who were there in the 1960s and '70s, are the best remembered of the recent licensees. After they moved to the Dragon in the early 1980s the Castle again changed hands several times, finally closing in about 1994. It subsequently saw service as an Indian restaurant before becoming a private house.

On a visit to Rome in 1821, Mary Dorothea Phillips, daughter of Nathaniel Phillips of Slebech Hall, met and fell in love with a romantic and dashing nobleman by the name of Charles Frederick de Rutzen. Heir to a large estate on the Baltic coast of Imperial Russia — now part of Lithuania — Baron de Rutzen spoke several languages fluently, was a first-class horseman and an excellent shot. After a whirlwind courtship, he and Mary were married in 1822 and the couple settled happily in fashionable Brighton. When her two brothers both died young and unmarried, Mary and her sister became co-heiresses. And in 1830, as Baroness de Rutzen, she moved back to Slebech Hall with her husband and growing brood of children.

The Baron and Baroness quickly began to make their presence felt around their new estate. They built an attractive bridge over the Cleddau at Blackpool Mill and later erected a new church at Slebech. A keen huntsman, the Baron imported wild boar from his homeland and released them in Canaston Wood — much to the annoyance of the local farmers. The Slebech estate also included much of the lower end of Narberth, and in 1831 the Baron began redeveloping a one-acre site in a prime position just south of the market square. Much of the eastern side of Market Street was demolished and prominent local architect James Hughes was given the job of replacing the old houses with a 'new and commodious market place' capable of accommodating 22 butchers, five fishmongers, 12 cheesemongers, 41 hawkers and 70 corn dealers.

Hughes based his design on that of Haverfordwest Market, but died in a riding accident before he could finish the commission. That task fell to another local architect called Thomas Rowlands who seems to have persuaded the Baron to set the market place some distance back from the street, along which would be built a smart new terrace including a coaching inn and five houses. The market opened in October 1832, followed the next

The coach arch at the Rutzen Arms with the Baron's name emblazoned above.

year by the **Rutzen Arms** — an imposing, three-storey building with the Baron's name emblazoned above one of the two coach-arches which gave access to the market and stables at the rear. Both enterprises were beset with problems from the outset. To start with, the traders and hawkers completely ignored the new market building and carried on displaying their produce in the streets — where there weren't any tolls to pay. And a surveyor who examined the inn and new houses came to the conclusion that they were so shoddily designed and built that the Baron would be within his rights not to pay the architect. Rowlands sued for payment, and the case rumbled on acrimoniously for several years.

Eventually, the inn began to flourish, with Martha Evans, formerly of the nearby Golden Lion, as the first licensee. Even the market place started to pick up trade — the hawkers having been driven off the streets by threats of legal action by the irate Baron. But the Rutzen Arms jinx still seems to have been in force, because Martha Evans left in strange circumstances in 1840. What happened is unclear, but the incident prompted Mrs. Evans' daughters to place a notice in the local press expressing their gratitude 'for the very liberal support experienced by their mother at the above establishment, which by undeserved and unexpected ill-treatment they were obliged to leave'.

The Evans girls went back to running the Golden Lion, whose landlord, David Philipps, replaced them at the Rutzen Arms. One of his first jobs was to turn the inn into temporary barracks for members of the Castlemartin Yeomanry who were stationed at the Rutzen Arms in the early 1840s to guard the local workhouse and Plaindealings turnpike gate against attacks by the Rebecca rioters. David Philipps was still in charge when he died in 1848; his death notice recorded the fact that he had been an innkeeper and auctioneer in Narberth upwards of 43 years. He was succeeded by his daughters, but in 1849 an advert appeared seeking new tenants to run the inn. 'The Misses Philipps, the present tenants, intend retiring from business having made their fortunes' claimed the advert, which added that 27 acres of rich meadowland adjoined the premises. The new tenant was James Pugh, son of Lewis Pugh who ran the Castle Inn at Haverfordwest. When he died in 1852 he was replaced by his daughter Elizabeth Pugh who in 1855 proudly presented a performance by Mr. Hoffmann's Organophonic Band in the assembly room at the inn; she was still running the inn in 1861.

Draper and publican Richard Phelps was the last to follow the well-trodden path from the Golden Lion to the Rutzen. He held the licence from 1865 until his death in 1877, while John Lewis from Tenby was the tenant for much of the 1880s. By this time the Rutzen was well established as a busy commercial inn and posting house, and its assembly room continued to be a popular venue for concerts and other entertainments. No sporting fixture or ploughing match was complete without dinner, toasts and speeches in the Rutzen Arms afterwards. The local freemasons also used the Rutzen; there was a spacious lodge-room behind the inn, and the masonic symbol of a square and compass can still be seen above the door next to the coach arch.

An article which appeared in the *West Wales Guardian* in 1935 recalled the Rutzen in its late Victorian hey-day and is worth repeating at length, not least for the light it sheds on the rigid class distinctions that once existed in the inns of Pembrokeshire.

> In addition to the sale of light refreshments, the proprietor usually kept 10 or 12 horses for posting, a bus met each train at the railway station, and on fair days and market days the large dining room was always full to capacity. The spacious assembly rooms were regularly appropriated for concerts and dramatic entertainments, and travelling entertainers always produced the 'show' there. In those days it was the weekly meeting place of magistrates, landowners, professional men and the larger agriculturalists and every Thursday the bar was thronged with those district magnates eagerly discussing the topics of the moment.
>
> In those circumstances it will be easily understood that the trade at the Rutzen was 'strictly select' and that people of the working classes rarely ventured within the sacred portals because they profoundly realised that the chance of being attended to would be definitely remote. With the passing of time this 'exclusion' at the hotel and its multiplicity of activities have largely disappeared. In my boyhood about 12 to 15 commercial travellers were put up each night and in the daytime they were driven around the countryside in conveyances obtainable at the hotel. On market and fair days about 100 horses were stabled. A large staff of indoor and outdoor servants was maintained and without doubt it was counted with the busiest residential and commercial hotels in west Wales.

William Davies was the innkeeper by 1891, while five years later — when Margaret Davies was licensee — the inn was sold to wine merchants James Williams by Albert Richard Francis Maximilien de Rutzen, son of the original de Rutzens of Slebech. The market place behind the inn was rebuilt in 1897 to serve both as a market house and public hall for the town. Called the Victoria Hall in honour of the Queen's jubilee, the building boasted state-

The view up Market Street on carnival day, 1906, with the Castle Inn on the left and the Rutzen Arms on the right.

of-the-art market stalls which could be closed up flush with the walls at night to allow social functions to take place. Entertainments in the newly-opened hall in 1897 included a performance of *Uncle Tom's Cabin* by 'a coloured troupe' and a week of 'theatrical representations' by Pepper's Ghost Company.

Margaret Davies remained in charge until 1903, while W.E. Jenkins — 'whose gifts in the direction of picturesque phrase have on more than one occasion been the delight and admiration of fellow townsmen' — was land-lord from 1906 to 1920. It is said that a regular visitor to the Rutzen at this time was a champagne company representative from Germany by the name of Manfred von Richthofen. As the 'Red Baron' he was to become the most feared German air ace of World War I.

Ernest Croucher held the licence in the early 1920s, while in 1925 the licence passed from the late Mr. David Morgan to his widow, Mrs. Lillie Morgan who was still overseeing the running of the inn in 1937. Charles Brady was in charge during the 1940s, and the war-time dances at the Rutzen were very popular, particularly as they offered a chance for local girls to meet the American servicemen who were stationed in the area. After the war, a refurbishment by James Williams meant that the Rutzen enjoyed a last flourish as an hotel, and in 1953 it played host to one of the first Pakistani cricket teams ever to tour Britain — the Pakistan Eagles — who played a couple of games in the county. The Victoria Hall, which had long been rented by the Borough Council for the use of the town, was put up for sale by James

The Castle and the Rutzen in the early 1950s.

Williams in 1947. It was half-expected that the council would purchase the hall, but when no bids were forthcoming by 1950 the firm turned it into a bottling plant and bottle store. The council realised too late that the town's only public hall had been taken away and the Queens Hall had to be built to replace it.

The Rutzen Arms itself closed for business in June 1957, although it didn't actually lose its licence until 1961. It was used by James Williams as a soft drinks store for a while, but gradually fell into disrepair after the company moved its operations to Spring Gardens. (The Victoria Hall bottle-works — the old market — was demolished in the 1970s). A Grade II listed building, the Rutzen was eventually rescued in the late 1980s when it was converted into flats, and a recent refurbishment has happily completed the job of restoring the former inn to its original handsome appearance.

The redevelopment of this street by the Baron de Rutzen meant the demolition of several buildings, some of which would have been ale-houses. These might have included the **Fishguard Arms** where David Williams was the landlord from 1822 to 1826 and the **Bolt-in-Tun** where Lewis Evans held the licence from 1822 to 1828. Evan Howell was landlord in 1830, in which year he was imprisoned for debt. The unusual name of this pub dates back to the Middle Ages and the use of old wooden barrels or 'tuns' for target practice by archers and crossbowmen. Such a barrel might then be retrieved and displayed as a tavern sign, often with the arrows still embedded.

The **Bush Tavern** was five doors up from the Rutzen and being in Market Square rather than Market Street it survived the redevelopment. Ann Roblin was the landlady in 1822 but a road surveyor named Thomas Thomas took over in 1823 and remained at the Bush for exactly 50 years, dying in harness in 1873 aged 84. A meeting place of the Narberth Friendly Society in the 1840s, the Bush was involved in an amusing incident which took place in 1842 and was reported in colourful detail in the *Welshman*:

> The inhabitants of Narberth were yesterday scared and astonished, delighted and affrighted, by the coming off of a most novel horse-race between their fat, well-conditioned rector and the evangelical curate of Newton and Yerbeston all round and through this dirty town.

The reporter went on to describe how the curate's 'cat-hammed, goose-rumped bay' was standing harnessed to a cart outside a building in Sheep Street — now St. James Street. The 18-stone rector, meanwhile, was seated upon his grey horse outside the Rose and Crown at the bottom of High Street. Suddenly the curate's horse took fright and charged off down the street. This in turn terrified the Rector's mount which set off up High Street 'firing his stern guns most rapidly'. Somehow the curate's horse managed to turn the corner into High Street and by the time the Angel was reached the terrified Rector could see 'death upon the pale horse' looming behind. The Rector swung right into Spring Gardens, the curate's runaway nag in hot pursuit. And then, at the last second, the Rector managed to swing into the Bushes Lane just as the curate's horse and cart went flying past.

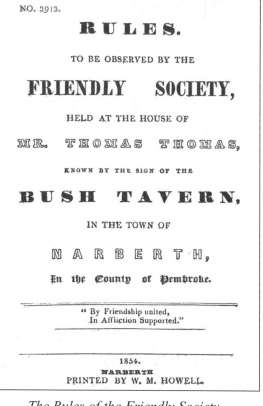

NO. 3913.

RULES.

TO BE OBSERVED BY THE

FRIENDLY SOCIETY,

HELD AT THE HOUSE OF

MR. THOMAS THOMAS,

KNOWN BY THE SIGN OF THE

BUSH TAVERN,

IN THE TOWN OF

NARBERTH,

In the County of Pembroke.

" By Friendship united,
In Affliction Supported."

1854.
NARBERTH
PRINTED BY W. M. HOWELL.

The Rules of the Friendly Society which met at the Bush in the 1850s.
Courtesy of the County Library, Haverfordwest.

The door of every house was occupied by its staring inhabitants as the cantankerous Rector quietly rode his grey back down Pig Street (High Street), mopping his red and ample face preparatory to cooling his heated intestines by a copious libation of the famous Narberth Ale at the Bush.

George Thomas, son of the long-serving Thomas, was landlord from 1873 until his death in 1887 when Thomas Eynon took over the licence. Miss Lilian Baker was the landlady from 1889 to 1891, but the Bush seems to have closed shortly after this date; in 2004 the building housed a shop known as 'Nomads'.

Pedlars and cheapjacks found a ready market for their wares in Narberth.

Above the Bush the road opens into the market square. Here, where the town stocks once stood, is where cheapjacks and pedlars would congregate on market days, together with farmers' wives with their baskets of eggs and butter, Llangwm oyster-women, dealers in tinware and crockery, local women selling cakes and buns and a host of other small-time traders. The official market hall may have been behind the Rutzen Arms, but this was where the real fun and the real bargains were to be found.

Nowadays the square is an open space, with the war memorial occupying a grassy triangle where the roads meet. However, up to the 1840s there was a cluster of buildings in the middle of the square, including the old market house and at least one pub. This was the **Talbot** in the narrow lane which was Old Market Street. Jane Harries was landlady in 1823 and Thomas Lewis ran

Narberth market in 1813 when there were buildings in the middle of the market square — including the Talbot Inn.

the pub between 1824 and 1835. In 1840 the freehold of the Talbot was up for sale, together with a piece of ground alongside known as 'The Old Market Place'. An advert for the property stated that the pub was 'lately occupied by Thomas Lewis as tenant at will, at the rent of £13 per annum'. It was bought by the Lloyd family of Lacques, Llansteffan, and Mary Protheroe appears to have been the landlady in the early 1840s. However the pub must have been demolished during the next decade, because a list of property owned by William Lloyd of Lacques at the time of his death in 1855 refers to 'the site of the Talbot Inn and the site of the Old Market Ground at the Cross'.

Facing onto the square at the bottom of St. James Street was the **White Hart Inn**, an old coaching inn with a stable yard reached by means of White Hart Lane which still runs alongside. There is a reference to this inn in 1776, but nothing else is known until a gentleman named James Williams took over the lease in 1797.

Following a ploughing match between farm servants held near Narberth in November 1808, their landowning employers 'sat down to an elegant dinner at the White Hart where the evening was most agreeably spent in conversation on agricultural subjects'. James Williams — who seems to have had no direct connection with the later wine and spirit merchants of the same name — ran the White Hart until his death in 1828, at which point his widow Eleanor took over the inn. She was still there in 1835 and the White Hart was still being recommended as the best inn in Narberth by Nicholson's *Cambrian Travellers' Guide* in 1840. However the guide was seriously out of date by this time, because the White Hart, having lost much of its trade to the Rutzen

A rare view of the White Hart when it was still a single property.
Picture courtesy of Mrs. Elizabeth Horne.

The White Hart has now been divided into two properties.

Arms, was in decline and may even have been forced to close for a while; there is a suggestion that it reopened in 1840 as a humble beer-house under the management of William Griffiths.

The building subsequently closed as an inn altogether, but was given a new lease of life when local wine and spirit merchant, grocer and hop dealer Evan Protheroe Lewis moved in and made it the centre of his various business activities. A fire in November 1846 caused considerable damage, but this was soon repaired and over the next couple of decades Mr. Protheroe Lewis became one of the town's most prominent businessmen. Descended from two notable local families, the Protheroes of Dolwilym and the Lewis family of Vron, Llandewi Velfrey, Mr. Protheroe Lewis seems to have inherited from them the gentry's love of cock-fighting. Although this sport was officially banned in 1835, it continued to take place 'behind closed doors' and it is believed that Mr. Protheroe Lewis maintained the old cock-pit behind the White Hart for the entertainment of himself and a few associates. On one occasion when the police raided the premises, Mr. Protheroe Lewis managed to keep them talking long enough for the participants (and their fighting cocks) to escape through the stable yards and over the roof tops to safety.

In later years the old White Hart became the private house of Mr. Protheroe Lewis and his large family, and in the early part of the 20th century it was divided into two properties, the original portico being replaced by twin front doors. During the course of renovations a few years ago, the remains of the former cock-pit were discovered at the rear of the premises.

Across the square was the **Globe** which opened in 1826 when it was run as a sideline by local shoemaker Thomas Upton — boot and shoe-making being a major cottage industry in Narberth at one time. He was still there in 1830, but the pub had changed hands by 1835 and was being run by Benjamin Phillips. Thomas Rees and his wife Rebecca had charge from 1840 to 1844, after which the property became a chemist's shop run by George James and later by David Jones. They kept up the licence in order to be able to sell spirit-based medicines, and no doubt a room at the back of the building continued to be used as a 'drinking den' for the select few.

This was certainly the case when chemist, seedsman, stationer and wine and spirit merchant James Lewis was the licensee in 1868. The Globe at this time was one of three 'chemist shop pubs' in the town — a source of much annoyance to the magistrates and the local temperance movement who felt that people going into the shops to buy their backache pills were being lured into the inner sanctum for a swift brandy. In 1872 the local magistrates took action against these pubs by refusing to renew any of the licences until the licensees made the drinking part of each building entirely separate from the shop. Mr. Lewis duly complied, but he died a couple of years afterwards, being succeeded by his widow Mrs. Margaret Lewis, while in April 1876 Evan John Howell took over the licence. Intriguingly, he also obtained consent 'to sell at the premises belonging to Nicholas Johns during the rebuilding of the Globe which was burnt'.

Benjamin Evans became the tenant in 1883 but when the licence came up for renewal in September 1884 it was refused; no reason for the refusal has come down to us. The Globe became a temperance hotel and was being run by boot-maker Thomas Sheldon in 1891, while there is a reference in 1928 to 'The Globe Boot and Shoe Store, Narberth' — another echo of its original use. It remained empty for several years before collapsing and being demolished in the early 1970s. It stood next door to the present chip shop.

Richard William Bell, a former licensed hawker, set himself up as a tea dealer in Market Square in the late 1830s. Shortly afterwards he began combining his tea business with running an ale-house known as the **Prince of Wales**. It was two doors below the Globe in 1841 but had closed by the 1850s.

The town's earliest recorded inn was the **Golden Lion** which was mentioned in 1753, although little is known about its early history. In 1809, the following advertisement appeared in the *Cambrian* newspaper:

> Lion Inn, Narberth, South Wales. David Philipps, truly sensible of the favours he has received since his commencement in business (for which he returns his most sincere thanks) and desirous of rendering his house still more commodious to his friends and others who may be inclined to favour him with their countenance and support, begs leave to inform them that he has lately rebuilt the said inn at a considerable expense whereby he has been enabled to put up for their accommodation a greater number

of extraordinary good beds and made other desirable alterations, and as he always lays in wines and liquors of the best quality and provides his stables, which are known to be excellent, with good hay and corn, he trusts his house will be found by Gentlemen Travellers and other as comfortable as any in South Wales.

The improvements may have included a cock-pit, because in 1818 the inn hosted a two-day festival of cock-fighting. The *Carmarthen Journal* reported that on the first day 'a Welsh main of 16 cocks was fought, and on the second day a main of cocks was fought between some gentlemen of Haverfordwest and some gentlemen of the neighbourhood of Narberth, which was won by the latter'.

Mr. Philipps remained landlord until 1820 and he was followed by Anthony Allen who kept the pub until 1828 when he left to run the Black Lion in Lampeter. The Golden Lion was then taken over by Martha Evans, and by 1832 she was advertising 'fine old wine and spirits, good stabling and lock-up coach-houses, a neat chaise and car, excellent horses and careful drivers' at the 'Lion Commercial Inn'. Having made such a success of the Lion, Martha Evans then left to run its newly-opened rival, the Rutzen Arms just down the hill.

In January 1835 David Philipps returned for another spell in charge, having spent some time at the Windsor Castle in Cold Blow. During his second stint the Lion became well known for its 'ordinaries' on fair and market days — an ordinary being a meal prepared at a fixed rate for all-comers. Philipps left again in 1840, also to run the Rutzen Arms, to be replaced by former licensee Martha Evans and her daughters Elizabeth and Caroline. The ladies took out an advertisement in the *Welshman* newspaper advising 'the Nobility, Gentry, Commercial Gentlemen, Farmers and the Public in General' that they were now running the Lion, 'which although not on so large a scale as the Rutzen is equal in comfort and accommodation'. Benefits of the Lion also included 'a well-known and experienced Hostler'.

Despite this, by 1842 the lease of the pub was being advertised once more in the local press. 'A rich meadow of land will be let with the inn if required', added the advert. Richard John was the new licensee, having previously run the King's Arms in Haverfordwest. James Pugh took over in December 1847, offering 'excellent accommodation, strict attention and moderate charges'; in 1849 he followed a well-trodden career path by taking over the Rutzen Arms. And as the Rutzen continued to cream off the trade, so an advert appeared in the *Welshman* in July 1850 to the effect that 'the old-established inn called the Lion, now converted into a capital shop and dwelling house' was for sale. It was local tradesman Richard Phelps who was responsible for turning the Lion into a drapery shop, but business must have been disappointing because in 1852 he put all of the stock up for sale and devoted his energies to reopening the Lion as an inn.

By December 1852 he was ready to relaunch the Lion, advertising that 'every branch connected with general innkeeping and commercial business will be promptly and efficiently conducted'. Nearly 50 gentlemen and tradesmen attended the housewarming dinner which marked the reopening of the inn, and when Mr. Powell's pack of hounds met outside the inn the following day, it meant that the Lion received the seal of approval from the local squirearchy. Encouraged by this, Richard Phelps went on to carry out improvements to the commercial and sitting rooms at the inn, 'which thereby offer every accommodation for commercial gentlemen'. It became the regular venue for the 'ordinary' which followed Narberth steeplechase meetings, held over land near Princes Gate, and Phelps remained as landlord of the Lion for more than ten years. Eventually, however, he too made the move to the Rutzen Arms and with his departure the Lion finally closed for good.

However it didn't lose its link with the licensed trade, since it was subsequently taken over by the enterprising James Williams who made it both his home and the headquarters of his successful business as a grocer and wine and spirit merchant. James Williams was born in 1819 at Kingswood farm on the outskirts of what was then the new town of Pembroke Dock. He was the third son of a tenant farmer — also named James Williams — and his wife Martha. Although it is impossible to be certain, since the name is such a common one, it appears that in 1827 the elder James Williams decided to combine farming with brewing. In his book *Pembroke People* Richard Rose reveals that in that year, James Williams of Pembroke Dock received a 160-gallon brewing copper from a firm in Bristol and that he was soon ordering hops for his new brewery from merchants in Oxfordshire. Unfortunately he subsequently found himself in serious difficulties due to what would now be called 'a cash flow crisis'. He was imprisoned for debt in 1828 and there is no sign of the brewery in the 1830 trade directory.

However, by 1830 one of the sons of James Williams of Kingswood was living in Market Square, Narberth. This was Arthur Williams, a grocer, draper and maltster whose malt-house is now an antiques warehouse. By 1840 he had given up the malting trade to concentrate on his grocery and drapery business, helped by his younger brother James who was lodging with him. Ten years later, the census reveals that Arthur had departed the scene leaving James Williams — master grocer, merchant and draper — in charge of the business.

The 1860s saw a major upturn in the fortunes of both James Williams and Narberth town itself. The railway arrived in 1866, and it appears that Williams was one of the first local businessmen to appreciate the opportunities that this opened up. He moved across the square to the former Golden

119

Lion where he he set himself up as a wine and spirit merchant, grocer and hop and seed dealer, aided by his equally business-like young wife Eliza, and soon the enterprise began to grow.

Although the company is often referred to as 'Narberth brewers' there seems no evidence that James Williams ever ran a brewery of his own; possibly his father's experiences had put him off that trade. Instead he began dealing with the big Burton breweries, ordering substantial quantities of beer and stout which arrived by rail in large wooden casks. This would then be decanted into bottles and smaller kegs and sold on to local pubs along with the wine and spirits which also arrived by rail to be stored in the 'spirit room' at the old Golden Lion. According to one account:

> The bottling process was carried on in two buildings, the ale in the cellars of the main building, the stout in a warehouse on the opposite side of the square. There were bottling and corking machines and the work provided employment for a number of girls who, in the fashion of the time, wore shawls and long skirts and flat caps.

As the business expanded, so the bottling process became increasingly efficient:

> It was said to be possible for twelve girls to label 240 dozen bottles an hour on a revolving table, and that a team of five could bottle on average 10 kilderkins (700 dozen) per day. All casks were to be tapped the night before bottling. Corks were never to be boiled as they would lose their elasticity; instead they were soaked in beer.

Other activities included the making of baskets to cover the stoneware jars in which some of the beer and spirits were sold, and a basket-maker was employed solely for this purpose, working in a special loft. The barrels of beer were stored in the Keg Yard at the back of the building, across Water Street, where there was also stabling for the horses which pulled the firm's drays. A further expansion of business came when the firm began to acquire its own portfolio of public houses, initially in the Narberth area but later further afield.

In March 1894 James Williams died, and his widow Eliza and son James Hamilton ('Jimmy') Williams carried on building up the family business until her death in 1904. This left Jimmy Williams as sole proprietor of the firm, and he soon showed himself to be an astute and progressive businessman. He built the Bonded Stores in Church Street, where much larger quantities of Scotch whisky, port, rum and sherry could be stored 'in bond', and he developed his own special spirit blends. James Williams' blended 'Glomore' whisky and 'Old Vatted Rum', sold in distinctive stoneware jars, soon became popular not just locally but all over Britain.

Many more public houses were acquired — over 70 in Pembrokeshire alone — and as the James Williams empire spread ever further in the 1920s thanks to the introduction of motor lorries, so depots were opened in Pembroke, Haverfordwest, Carmarthen and Cardigan to supply the tied houses — and many free houses — with kegs of beer and bottles of wine, spirits, beer and stout. All the firm's operations continued to be controlled from the former Golden Lion and from various adjoining premises, and soon the firm could lay claim to being the biggest wholesale wine and spirit merchants in west Wales.

Even running such a large and successful enterprise wasn't enough for the energetic Jimmy Williams, a World War One veteran and a noted sportsman in his younger days, and he was forever coming up with schemes which he thought would benefit trade and the community. Chief among these was electric lighting, and after he had successfully overseen the change from gas lighting to electricity in Narberth, he pushed through similar schemes in Pembroke and Haverfordwest. He also tried his hand at market gardening and was an avid writer of long letters to the local press on a variety of subjects.

Sadly, a perceived lack of enthusiasm for his ambitious projects began to depress Mr. Williams, as did the national downturn in trade in the late 1920s and the consequent hardships being experienced at that time. His health began to suffer as a result of this depression, and in August 1930 he committed suicide by shooting himself with a revolver. He was 63 and had never married.

The firm subsequently became a limited company known as James Williams (Narberth), with Mr. Hendrick Howell — a cousin of Jimmy Williams — as managing director. Mr. Howell was succeeded in 1964 by his nephew, Mr. John Lee-Davies and later by Mr. Desmond Wilson. By the 1980s, the buildings around the Market Square had outlived their usefulness, especially as the

The former Golden Lion.

121

delivery lorries had to collect from four different sites — the keg yard, the spirit store at the former Golden Lion, the bottling store at the old Victoria Hall and the soft drinks store at the former Rutzen. Purpose-built premises were opened on the outskirts of town to incorporate all of these activities under one roof and the Golden Lion's long connection with the licensed trade came to an end.

In the 1840s, Thomas Collins occupied a house just below the Golden Lion. A gentleman of that name was landlord of the **Red Cow** in Narberth between 1822 and 1826, but no other information has come to light. Another pub which may have stood near here was the **Pelican** which David Collins ran from 1835 to 1840; this may have been the unnamed beer-shop which Ann Collins ran in the early 1850s.

This marvellous photograph, which dates from the late 1860s or early 1870s, shows the Cross Inn, next door to the Court House, when William Harwood was the licensee.

Picture courtesy of Narberth Museum.

On the south side of the Church Street / Market Street junction, was the **Cross**, which was originally a beer-house when it was run by John Phillips in the 1840s and early '50s. The landlord from 1858 to 1875 was William Harwood, a painter and decorator by trade, and it was during his day that the original pub was demolished and a new pub built a little further down Market Street. The reason for this was the construction of the town's imposing court-house in 1864 which took over the site of the original Cross Inn. William Harwood was succeeded by his widow Mary Ann Harwood, while Benjamin Morris was there from 1880 to 1884. The pub appears to have closed in about 1895 and later became the premises of Hubert V. Thomas, cabinet maker. It is now a private house.

122

CHAPTER TEN

Narberth
CHURCH STREET & WATER STREET

'Church Street is a disgrace to any civilised town', declared the *Narberth Parish Magazine* in 1897. 'Refuse of all kinds covers the roadway, whilst the so-called pavement is used as a convenient resting place for the carts of the parish, thus compelling foot passengers to use the filthy street'. The author of this diatribe was the Rev. John Morris who probably had more cause than most to grumble, since the street led from centre of town to his church.

Close to the church is the bonded warehouse, built for James Williams at the beginning of the 20th century, where large amounts of spirits were kept 'in bond'. The door of this warehouse had two padlocks. One key was kept by the warehouse manager and the other by the local Excise officer and twice a week they would meet at the store, unlock the two padlocks and check out the requisite amount of whisky, rum etc. The bonded store closed following the company's move to the edge of town and there are plans to convert it into a museum.

The Bonded Stores may be converted to a museum.

The pubs in the street were clustered around the junction with Water Street, where there was a hostelry on both corners. On the eastern corner was the **Dolphin** where Jacob Thomas was the landlord between 1810 and 1835 and a widow named Mrs. Esther Thomas

The house on the left of this photograph was built on the site of the old Painters' Arms. The tall building next to it was once the Court House inn.

held the licence from 1840 to 1851. By 1858 it was being run by publican and painter John Thomas who duly renamed it the **Painters' Arms** and remained in charge for some ten years.

By 1871 the licensee was John M. Thomas, a 28-year-old builder and cabinet maker. It was John M. who redeveloped this corner of town during the early 1870s, replacing the Painters' Arms with an elaborate private house which he built for himself out of dressed limestone and which he named 'Rock House'. Alongside this property he built the **Court House**, an ambitious pub-cum-hotel named in honour of the splendid new court-rooms opposite. Mr. Thomas briefly ran the inn himself before leasing it to John Prickett. He didn't stay very long, setting the pattern for the next 20 years as William Jones, James Savage, Elizabeth George, Percy Baker, Eliza Williams, Frederick Lewis and Stephen Thomas all came and went. It became part of the James Williams empire, but was regularly targeted for closure by the police, being finally declared redundant by the magistrates in February 1919 with £256 being paid out in compensation. The fact that the pub possessed little or no stabling was a factor in its demise, while the high turnover of licensees can't have helped.

On the other corner of the junction with Water Street stands the present-day **Eagle.** This began life as the **Ball** and was kept by James Phillips and his wife Sarah from 1810 to 1846 when James died at the age of 73. A map dated 1849 showed the pub still being called the Ball, but this changed the following year when a new landlord took over. John Davies had previously run the original Eagle inn further along Church Street, and he must have liked the name because the Ball was soon rechristened the Eagle, while his former pub became the Old Eagle. John Davies and his wife Jane were popular licensees and remained in charge throughout the 1860s when the pub was the headquarters of a friendly society known as the Sympathetic

Benefit Society and the Davies' catered for 100-strong meetings of the organisation.

In 1871 the owner and licensee was George Henry Evans while John Thomas (the third local publican of that name) took over in 1877, having moved from the Providence Inn on the road to Templeton. It proved an eventful few years for the licensee, beginning in September 1881 when he made history by becoming the first landlord in Pembrokeshire to be prosecuted for contravening the new Welsh Sunday Closing Act. However the case against him was dismissed when it was pointed out to the red-faced police prosecutor that the new law didn't come into force until October 10.

In 1884 the Eagle was nearly destroyed by fire. One afternoon a customer from up-country entered the pub with a container of benzolene which he placed under a table. It being market day, and the pub packed to the gills, it was inevitable that the container should be kicked over. The benzolene ignited and soon the bar was a mass of flames as the terrified customers fled into the street. The fire was eventually brought under control — but not before the bar and fittings had been completely destroyed.

No-one seems to have been hurt in the blaze, but John Thomas died a few months later at the age of 39, the licence being transferred to his widow Ellen. Then, in 1887, the licence passed to James Bevan who ran the pub until

The Eagle on the corner of Water Street and Church Street in about 1928.

Picture courtesy of Narberth Museum.

his death in 1895 when he too was succeeded by his widow, Sophia. Mrs. Eliza Jones was the landlady between 1901 and 1916, followed by George Andrews. John Wheeler Davies kept the pub from 1923 until his death in 1930, after which the Eagle was run by his widow Eleanor Margaret until 1940.

Bessie Denham ran the pub during the war, while post-war licensees included Elizabeth Jordan, Tommy Tucker and Mr. Fred Harris — 'Fred the Eagle' — who ran the pub with his wife Beryl from 1965 until the early 1970s. Tragically the Eagle was then the scene of another serious fire in which one of the Harris' children died. James Williams, who owned the pub, rebuilt it after the fire, since when it has changed hands on a fairly regular basis. The Eagle is still thriving, although with its subdued lighting, poster-covered walls and soundtrack of thumping rock music it is unrecognisable from the market day local that country people would have known 100 years ago.

The Eagle as it looked in 2001, having been rebuilt following fire damage in the early 1970s.

The original Eagle inn was more or less next door, just along Church Street. George Edwardes was the landlord of this long-established inn from 1824 until his death, aged 62, in 1836, and Margaret Edwardes, presumably his widow, was licensee in 1840. A hatter called John Davies took over soon afterwards, but, as we have seen, when he moved to the nearby Ball ten years later he took the pub sign with him.

The Eagle perforce became the **Old Eagle**, and the landlord from 1851 to 1881 was the one-legged Daniel Evans (his other leg was amputated by a surgeon in 1854 'in just two minutes' following a mining accident). Owned by the Cresselly estate, this pub was always a very busy place on market days with stabling for dozens of horses. It was also said to be the last pub in Narberth still selling beer produced on the premises, despite being in the shadow of the James Williams empire.

James Eynon took over in the late 1880s and ran the Old Eagle for over 45 years, purchasing the pub, stables, garden and outbuildings from the Cresselly estate for £300 in 1892. He retired following the death of his wife, Mrs. Esther Eynon, in August 1934, and enjoyed a happy retirement, finally expiring in 1953 at the age of 88.

The former Old Eagle in Church Street.

Throughout his many years at the Old Eagle the pub had an unblemished reputation, but it seems to have gone downhill after he left. It was run for a couple of years by Walter Heaven, and when he departed to run the Brewery Inn at Cosheston, David Morgan Edwards was granted a temporary licence. Edwards had previously been the landlord of the Three Horseshoes in Landshipping until that pub had been closed under the redundancy ruling. The Narberth police were soon grumbling that under Edwards' landlordship 'a certain class of individual of a rather undesirable type' had begun to assemble at the Old Eagle. The police opposed Edwards' application for a full licence and gave him such a hard time that he quit in 1936 and took a job as a farm labourer. The Old Eagle was sold soon afterwards and became a private house; happily it still bears the old pub name.

In November 1812, John Allen, squire of Cresselly, turned up in Narberth. As parliamentary candidate for the united boroughs of Wiston, Pembroke and Tenby he was keen to canvass as many votes as possible in the town. It was reported in the *Carmarthen Journal:* 'A great number of the united Burgesses assembled at the **New Inn** when they distributed an ample portion of good ale between the well-wishers of Mr. A.' The 1849 map shows a pub called the New Inn four doors along from the Old Eagle, nowadays part of the corner building where the slope ends and the road to the church narrows. Since most of the property in this area belonged to the Cresselly estate at the time, it is likely that this was the inn where Squire Allen tried to buy his votes. Thomas Parry is recorded as running the New Inn from 1822 to 1840, followed by Thomas Mathias between 1844 and 1850.

Water Street, which links Church Street with High Street, can still boast a remarkably high percentage of pubs in a short street. Just up from the Eagle is the **Dragon** which seems to have begun life in 1826 as a chemist and druggist business run by John Griffiths. By 1840 he had been joined in the business by John Nicholas and was selling wine and spirits, while by the time Thomas Smyth took over in the 1850s, a tiny beer and spirit shop at the rear of the premises was well established under the name of **Green Dragon**. Although unheated, with a bare stone floor, and just a counter and a couple of benches by way of furnishings, this little back-room drinking den was a favourite gathering place of the town's well-to-do tradesmen in the 1860s — a sanctuary from the market day hurly-burly of the other pubs in town.

However, as has been seen elsewhere, these 'chemist shop pubs' were a tremendous irritant to the temperance brigade. Attempts to close the Green Dragon began in 1865, and in 1872 the local magistrates refused to renew the licence until Smyth made the drinking part of the house entirely separate from the shop. But unlike the other local chemists who meekly complied with the ruling, Smyth appealed against this decision at the Quarter Sessions in Haverfordwest and managed to win his case. There were remarkable scenes of celebration in Narberth when this verdict was announced, Smyth being a popular sort of chap (he had chaired the meeting in May 1869 that led to the formation of Narberth United Cricket Club; he was an angler of repute, a successful racehorse owner and a thorn in the side of pompous bureaucracy). On his return from court, Smyth was carried shoulder high around the town, fireworks were exploded and a large tar-barrel was set alight on the Town Moor. He remained licensee of the Green Dragon

Tommy Nicholas advertises the Dragon Stores in 1957.

until 1885 and died in 1892 during an influenza epidemic.

Thomas James was licensee in 1889 while Thomas Parsell Roberts ran the pub in tandem with a grocery business from 1897 to 1901. It appears to have dropped the 'Green' part of its name around this time, although the *Welshman* newspaper in May, 1898, reported that a meeting of the Hearts of Oak benefit society was held at the 'Green Dragon, Narberth'. By 1905 it had become a James Williams house and Frederick Nicholas ran the combined pub and grocery business from 1908 to 1928 followed by Mrs. Edith Nicholas who was still

A recent view of the Dragon in Water Street.

there in 1950. At some stage the two enterprises were separated, with the grocery side of the concern being moved to a shop on the Market Square while the Dragon became an out-and-out pub.

There exists an excellent description of the Dragon as it was before the Second World War and which shows that the old *sanctum sanctorum* was still in evidence.

> The room fronting on to the main street was very much a public bar for working men, but the back bar was an exclusive gentlemen's club for Narberth's professional classes. There the businessmen would gather for a drink round a table loaded with home boiled ham, pork pies, a dish of tomatoes, a loaf of bread and a pound block of farm butter. They ate as much as they wanted and then paid as much as they thought suitable by throwing shillings into the honesty kitty.

Best remembered of the Dragon licensees was undoubtedly Tommy Nicholas who was landlord from 1950 to 1972, while Ken Rees held the licence from 1973 to 1979 and Mike Griffin was landlord in the early 1980s. The pub lost some of its unique character when it was extensively remodelled by James Williams in the late 1980s to create the obligatory 'open plan' effect, but it remains a popular town centre local where licensee Ann Davies has been in charge since 1990.

The Barley Mow in Water Street, pictured in 2001.

As this book was being prepared for publication, there were signs that the **Barley Mow** in Water Street had closed for good. An old-established pub, it had half a dozen landlords during its first 150 years — and something like one a year in its last 15. From 1822 to 1854 the landlord was Thomas Hughes who was nearly 90 when he gave up the pub. A widow named Margaret Mathias took over and she was still serving in 1871 when she was 70. Thomas Edward Thomas held the licence from 1873 to 1882, followed by his widow Mrs. Margaret Thomas in 1891. She then married Richard Cook Davies who had a long stint as landlord, running the pub from 1895 to 1921 after which Margaret Davies carried on until 1933.

Licensee from 1934 to 1955 was Margaret Hall (this pub seems to have attracted Margarets), while other post-war licensees have included David and Dilys Hughes and Mrs. Catherine Mullens. In recent years the Barley Mow changed hands on a regular basis, underwent various internal alterations, and was shut from time to time; sadly the present closure looks like being the last.

CHAPTER ELEVEN

Narberth
HIGH STREET & BACK LANE

Once known as Pig Market Street, High Street has long been the main commercial thoroughfare of the town, being the route taken by the mail coaches. Many thriving family businesses were established along here, from grocers, drapers and ironmongers to watchmakers, chemists and cabinet-makers. All these business people must have viewed the regular livestock fairs with mixed feelings; they brought plenty of customers into town, but the tethering of animals along either side of the street was fraught with problems and many premises would erect temporary barriers to prevent the intrusion of curious cattle.

The town hall was in High Street, and it was here that the local magistrates court was held. In 1854, the Rev. Joseph Romilly attended the special sitting of the court held for the purpose of licensing the town's publicans. It seems to have been a very civilised affair, the magistrates — a doctor, a clergyman and a local squire — receiving 'a green bottle of sherry and a bag of biscuits' as a present from the assembled victuallers.

Many of the town's inns were in High Street, chiefly on the east side where Back Lane provided access to stable yards. And it was on this side of the street, on the corner of Market Square, that the **Rose and Crown** stood for many years. William Humphrey Evans was the long-serving landlord, running it as a pub and spirit shop from 1810 to 1837. In that year the 'established and compact inn' was put up for sale by auction, the ground floor comprising 'a large and commodious shop', together with parlour, sitting-room, kitchen and back kitchen. There were two bedrooms and a dining room on the floor above as well as five bedrooms on the second floor and four rooms in the attic. A six-stalled stable, dairy, coal-house and garden belonged to the inn and were located nearby, probably in Back Lane.

At this time the Rose and Crown was a regular stopping place for Royal Mail coaches travelling between London and Milford and also the *Cambrian* and *Regulator* passenger coaches which operated a summer shuttle-service between Haverfordwest and Carmarthen. Benjamin Phillips was the landlord in the 1840s and he also acted as a spirit merchant while his widow, Jane Phillips, ran the business until her death in 1858. Licensee in 1861 was attorney's clerk John Phillips who died in 1873 aged 37; during his day the side door of the pub was the favoured market pitch of 'Liza the Cakes' whose robust buns and pies were a great favourite with hungry visitors to the market.

The 1874 licensee was Edmund Buckby who died two years later to be replaced by his widow Jane, and from 1881 to 1898 the landlord was John Rogers Ormond, who appears to have married the widow. She also outlived her second husband, because from 1898 until her death in 1901 the licensee was Mrs. Jane Ormond. The Rose and Crown was involved in a court case in 1883 when local bobby P.S. James charged John Ormond with serving on a Sunday. However the case was dropped in odd circumstances when Sergeant James refused to name the place in which he had been lurking while spying on the premises.

William John kept the pub from 1910 to 1914, while in 1918 licensee Charlotte Jones was fined the hefty sum of £15 for serving out of hours; her

customer was described as 'Albion Hammar, an alien, lumber camp, Wiston'. The pub, which often went by the nick-name 'The Gin Shop', had lost most of its former glory by this time and it closed the following year. It is now a butcher's shop.

Almost opposite the Rose and Crown, on an 'island' between High Street and Water Street, was the **Old Conduit**, the name

The Rose and Crown has been a butcher's shop for many years.

deriving from the spring of fresh water which rose nearby to give the town its water supply (and which, presumably, also accounted for the name of Water Street). Thomas Thomas kept the Old Conduit from 1822 to 1828 followed by William Peters in 1830, John Allen in 1835 and Sarah Thomas from 1840 to 1844. A carpenter named Thomas James appears to have been the last landlord of the Old Conduit, running it from about 1848 until his

The later Conduit Inn can be seen to the right of the Golden Sheaf in this late 19th-century view.
Picture courtesy of Narberth Museum.

death in November 1852 at the age of 68. The building survived in increasingly dilapidated state until the 1960s when it was one of several removed to create the Charles Salmon Memorial Garden.

The **Commercial Tavern** was opened in 1827 by John Thomas, and an innkeeper of that name appears on the 1841 census in High Street, a couple of doors above the Rose and Crown. His widow Margaret was in charge by 1850 but the pub seems to have closed shortly afterwards.

Moving further up the right hand side of the street, the building immediately below the Golden Sheaf gallery was once the **New Conduit**. The first reference to a pub of that name was in a newspaper report of 1848 which recounted how a thunderstorm had broken 30 panes of glass in the pub windows. A widow named Mary Griffiths ran the New Conduit from 1858 to 1881, during which time she regularly catered for meetings of the Victoria Benefit Society. John Davies took over in December of that year and ran the Conduit until his death in the early 1890s. His widow Mrs. Martha Davies remained landlady until 1909, and James Hughes was in charge from 1911 to 1918.

In that year Mr. Hughes was convicted of 'permitting drunkenness' at the Conduit, a charge which he strenuously denied. After being fined £2 he told the magistrates: 'I entered the licensed trade at 22, I am now 57 and I have never had a complaint against me. If you don't think I'm qualified to conduct the house, I'll take the sign down!' Which he did, tearing down the inn sign and giving up the licensed trade there and then. (According to one version of the story he went to work at the Rectory, looking after the pigs). The building became the Conduit Refreshment Rooms and lodging house and the premises later housed a grocery business — the Conduit Stores. Traces of the old pub were still visible as recently as the early 1980s, including the old bench seats in the back parlour and a primitive gents' urinal in the back yard, but the whole building was given a make-over in 1985. It has been suggested that the Golden Sheaf Gallery itself may once have been the pub called the **Wheatensheaf** which Griffith Davies kept from 1822 to 1827.

On the opposite side of the road was the **King's Arms,** which, as an advertisement once pointed out, was 'largely patronised by farmers, dealers and the general public as it occupies a splendid position in the centre of fairs and markets'. (Edwardian postcards show just how central the inn was, with cattle tethered on the pavement outside). The first known licensee was Lewis Edwardes, who was there from 1822 to 1826, but Henry Evans took over in 1828 and his name was still over the door 30 years later.

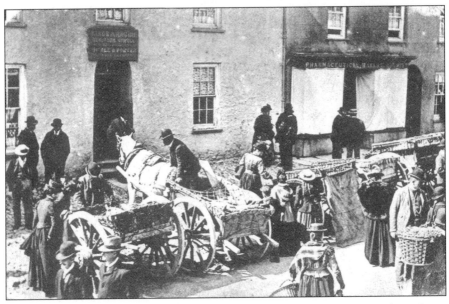

Plenty of bargains to be had outside the King's Arms in Narberth in the days when Benjamin Howell was licensee.

The King's Arms was owned by the Cresselly estate, and in October 1868 it was reported: 'Lady Catherine Allen's tenants in Narberth were regaled with their annual dinner at the King's Arms on Friday last'. It was the last such occasion before her son, Henry Seymour Allen, came of age, so Lady Catherine of Cresselly House sportingly invited all the tenants to take a glass of 'grog' with her. Ann Evans was licensee at the time, having run the pub since the death of her husband Henry in about 1860.

By the 1890s the King's Arms comprised a bar, tap-room, kitchen and larder on the ground floor, with two bedrooms and a dining room on the first floor and six bedrooms on the second floor. Benjamin Howells from Robeston Wathen held the licence between 1871 and 1905, having married Mary Evans, daughter of the previous licensees. Following his death, his widow kept the pub for a short time, after which it was altered with the addition of a couple of bay windows at the front and became a temperance hotel. The King's Arms remained a temperance hotel for a number of years before becoming a private house; it is now divided into two shops.

Two Narberth pubs with an entwined history are the Swan and the Old Swan. Rees Brown was running the **Swan** in 1822, but David Jenkins took over the following year and ran the pub until 1827. In that year he moved

The King's Arms after it had been given a facelift and had become a temperance hotel. The building on the right was once the Swan Inn.
Picture courtesy of the Narberth Museum.

135

across the road to new premises and took the sign with him, the new Swan being located next door to the King's Arms. David Jenkins was still there in the early 1830s, but John Phillips had taken over by 1835 and he was the landlord when the story of the Swan took another twist.

In 1838 the Baptists were looking for somewhere to build a chapel in Narberth, the cause having outgrown its earlier meeting house. They appealed to the Allens of Cresselly for a patch of land on which to build a chapel, and according to *Baptist Historical Sketches of Pembrokeshire*:

> J.H. Allen Esq., Cresselly, offered them one of the best sites in the middle
> of the town for the purpose, also a place for burial, together with several
> houses adjoining for £600.

An indenture dated 1838 shows that one of these buildings was the Swan occupied by John Phillips, and the chapel seems to have been built in part of the pub garden.

John Phillips left soon afterwards, presumably to run the Cross Inn below the Market Square, and James and Elizabeth Davies were in charge by 1844. They were still there in the harsh winter of 1854-55 when the pub was used as a soup kitchen for the poor of the parish. Later in 1855 the pub was broken into twice in a short space of time and quite large sums of money stolen. 'A strong opinion prevails that the two robberies have been committed by the same person', declared the *Pembrokeshire Herald* sagely. It was a meeting place of the Odd Fellows, whose 100 local members had a lodge room at the inn in the 1840s and '50s, and also of the rather more parochial St. James' Friendly Society.

By 1863 the licensee was David Rees, but for some reason he had his licence suspended for misconduct in 1869. The premises later became a chemist's shop, run initially by John Nicholas and then for many years by Ben Havard. In recent years the building has been occupied by Dickman's store.

When Mr. Jenkins left the original Swan in 1827 it seems to have been taken over by a widow named Mary Jenkins and renamed the **Old Swan**. She was still there in 1835 but the pub must have closed fairly soon afterwards. The Old Swan was part of the Narberth estate of the Lloyd family of Lacques, Llansteffan, and was situated across the road from the Swan at 18 High Street; by 2004 the premises had become Wisebuys.

There is a reference to the **Black Horse** in 1818 when the occupier was David William Glover, while William Davies kept the pub in 1822. Richard Thomas took over the licence the following year and was still there in 1826. In that year the sale took place of the 'dwelling house and premises previously owned by Richard Thomas, innkeeper' together with brew house, yard and stables. However by January 1828, when the pub was again put up for sale by auction, the licensee was John Davies who paid an annual rent of £15.

It is believed that the pub subsequently became the **Plough** which stood a few doors up from the Old Swan at 14 High Street and where the landlord from 1840 to 1861 was Philip Thomas. This pub had a history of minor fire damage. In November 1873 the brewhouse at the back of the inn was burnt to the ground, despite the best efforts of 'Mr. Smyth and his celebrated fire engine'. Londoner John Toohig was the landlord then, and he was still there in 1903, having escaped unscathed when another fire damaged the premises in February 1887. Arthur Berkley Williams was licensee from 1904 until his death in 1910 when the licence passed to his widow Margaret. The pub was closed under the redundancy ruling in 1917 when the owner was Mr. William Toohig and the licensee was David Davies who had been there since 1914. Pleading against the loss of his licence, Mr. Davies told the magistrates: 'I put up dealers on fair days'. But the fact that the Plough could only offer overnight accommodation for four men and one horse made it an obvious target for closure. It is now the offices of F.B. Mason, estate agents.

The **Farmers' Arms** once 'abutted' the Black Horse according to a lease dated 1825 — although on which side isn't known. In 1832 it was recorded that Mr. Thomas Thomas had died at the Farmers' Arms 'in the prime of his life' — possibly he was the chap who had previously run the Old Conduit. The landlord in 1835 was James Williams while The Samaritan Lodge of the True Ivorites met here in 1842. William James, clerk to Tenby solicitor John Gwynne, was the landlord from 1840 until his death in 1846 when the pub seems to have closed.

Two doors up from the Plough was the **Railway Tavern** which had its stables in Back Lane. Saddler James Phillips was the licensee from 1848 to 1858. It subsequently became a butcher's shop run for many years by Henry Edwards. And two doors further along was the short-lived **Commercial Inn**. John and Charlotte Meyrick were there from 1851 to 1853; they later ran the Burton Brewery pub in Dimond Street, Pembroke Dock.

Across the road, a few doors up from the Swan, was the **New Inn**. John Roblin and his wife Elizabeth ran a beer-house at this address in the 1850s before moving to the Ivy Bush, while the landlord from 1868 to 1891 was Benjamin Phillips from Wiston. The pub had closed by 1895 and by 2004 had become a Chinese restaurant.

The only surviving pub on this side of the street is the **Angel**, a long-established coaching inn which once had a stable yard where the Queens Hall now stands. The inn may have been kept by William Nicholas in 1784

The Angel in Narberth during its days as a Temperance Hotel.

A view of the Angel in the 1960s.
Picture courtesy of the *Western Telegraph.*

and Priscilla Nicholas in 1795, but the first licensee we can be sure about was David Smith Nicholas, who kept the Angel between 1810 and 1844. In 1840 an inquest was held at the inn into the death of William Scourfield of Robeston Wathen. The verdict that he had died from excessive drinking provided a lot of ammunition for the local temperance cause. The licensee from 1848 to 1861 was Rachael Nicholas, widow of the former land-lord, and in 1852 she catered for a get-together of a Friendly Society known as the Narberth Sympathetic Society. 'The evening was spent with the greatest hilarity', according to one account. Behind the bar between 1867 and 1874 was David Thomas Rhys, and in the 1880s Narberth cricket club used the inn as its head-quarters. There was another Friendly Society based here by this time — the Angel Club and Benefit Society — and an old photograph shows that it must have been run as a temperance hotel for a time.

Licensee from 1877 until his death in 1891 was builder George Harries. He built the three houses just above the Queens Hall origi-

The Angel as it looked in 2001, having grown to include the house on the left.

nally known as Woodbine Terrace, but now numbers 44, 45 and 46 High Street. His widow Mrs. Tirzah Harries was in charge until 1899, after which it became a James Williams house. From 1908 to 1921 the landlord was John Wheeler Davies, later of the Eagle, while Thomas Waters ran the pub between 1922 and 1935. It then became a Hancocks house under Mr. William Harries who remained in charge until 1952. Harold Griffiths was licensee for the next ten years, followed by Cyril Colman and then Wing Cdr. George Nelson Edwards, who began the task of modernising and refurbishing the inn in 1973 before moving to run the Swan in Little Haven for many years. These improvements were carried on in the 1970s and '80s by Eifion and Elsie Evans, and a private house just below the Angel was incorporated into the building, greatly adding to the size and facilities of the present inn.

Across the road on the eastern side of High Street was the **Welcome to Town.** An inquest was held there in 1848 into the death of a local serving woman who had drunk a glass of milk laced with hemlock. Whether it was murder, suicide or an accident remained a mystery. Landlord from 1840 to 1861 was horse-breaker David Gibby who shortly afterwards moved to open the Cresselly Arms at the southern edge of town.

Carpenter and joiner Isaac Thomas took over and renamed the pub the **Carpenters' Arms.** He remained the landlord until the pub closed in 1904 — a stint of nearly 40 years — and the old pub sign is preserved in the town museum. It reads:

Carpenters Arms
Isaac Thomas
Licensed retailer of all
Beers, Porters, Wine.
Not to sell on Sundays.

In the 1890s the **Ivy Bush**, next door up from the Carpenters' Arms, was the headquarters of a newly-constituted trade union, the Narberth and District Weavers' Society, which did its best to obtain better pay and conditions for workers at the local woollen mills — without a lot of success. It was a popular little pub on fair days and market days and was traditionally the place

A view of the Ivy Bush in 2002.

where country people from the Llawhaden area would gather when the trading was over. The first mention of a pub in Narberth called the Ivy Bush is in 1844, when John Webb was the landlord. He appears to have been succeeded in the 1850s by John Roberts, while by 1861 the licensees were currier John Roblin and his wife Elizabeth. Mr. Roblin must have died a few years later, because between 1867 and 1869 the licensee was Elizabeth Roblin. She then married a Scotsman named John Grierson and they continued to run the Ivy Bush for a few years before being succeeded by Benjamin John and his wife Margaret. From 1882 to 1900 the landlord was John Griffiths. He was followed by David Williams who was threatened with losing his licence in 1903 unless the back door of the pub was nailed shut. (In those days magistrates were more worried about people sneaking into pubs on a Sunday than any possible fire hazards).

By 1911 the Ivy Bush was a James Williams house and their tenant until 1918 was John Harries. Annie Davies was the landlady from 1919 to 1937, but the brewery seems to have had problems finding a settled tenant during and after the war and eventually sold the pub. Cyril Colman was there during the 1950s before moving to the Angel in 1962, making way for Jack and Lil Davies who ran the pub for the next ten years. Matt Barnes, who was licensee in the 1970s, made a number of internal alterations to the premises and for a while the Ivy Bush even had an upstairs restaurant. For the past 15 years the pub has been in the same family, being run initially by Mr. and Mrs. Fred Fox and later by their daughter and son-in-law Sue and John Cadwallader.

During refurbishment work at the house immediately above the Ivy Bush in 1984 a blocked-up doorway was discovered in the wall between the house and the pub, at second storey level. It is thought that on fair days and market days, when the town was busy, the accommodation at the Ivy Bush would be increased by using the neighbouring property as an overspill area. (Similar blocked-up doorways have been discovered elsewhere in the town).

The **Coach and Horses** on the corner is one of the most recent of the Narberth pubs to close, becoming a confectionery shop in 2003. Its early history is a little confusing, but George Edwards or Edwardes was landlord of a pub called the Coach and Horses in Narberth in 1823 while blacksmith William John was at the Coach and Horses in 1827. He seems to have changed the name of the pub to the **Unicorn**, under which sign it existed throughout the 1830s.

Ann Roblin, formerly of the Bush Tavern, took over in about 1840. Unlike most of the Roblin family, who were leather-workers and curriers, she was a carrier by trade, operating a small fleet of wagons and coaches between Narberth, Tenby and Haverfordwest. She restored the original name, evidently thinking it more appropriate, and carried on running the Coach and Horses until the mid 1860s when John Williams took over. In 1871 the pub was the scene of a dreadful accident when a woman working in the brew-house fell into the vat of boiling drink. 'She suffered for a week before she died,' reported the local paper with rather morbid relish.

John Williams' daughter Miss Esther Williams was in charge for a few years, but in 1876 the pub was taken over by Thomas Thomas who ran it with his wife Rachel until 1900; the 1881 census stated that the unfortunate Mr. Thomas was 'dumb'. For a few years around the turn of the century the

An artist's drawing of the unspoilt interior of the Coach and Horses in 1982.

Picture courtesy of Narberth Museum.

landlord was Benjamin Phillips — the third person of that name to hold a licence in High Street — but this was only a temporary measure because the pub remained in the Thomas family and from 1904 to 1955 the long-serving innkeepers were Mr. and Mrs. Arthur Evan Thomas, Arthur being the youngest son of the earlier licensees.

The regular meeting place of the Narberth quoits club in the 1900s, the Coach and Horses came within a whisker of losing its licence in 1917 when Mr. Thomas was convicted of selling a single

The Coach and Horses pictured in 1982.

Picture courtesy of Narberth Museum.

*The Coach and Horses as it looked in 2003,
not long before it closed.*

glass of beer outside permitted hours. This being wartime, the magistrates were inclined to be strict with publicans who broke the law and several worthies on the local bench were in favour of shutting down the pub on the strength of that one minor infringement. That the Coach and Horses was spared was due in large measure to the fact that the inn possessed plenty of stabling for horses on market day — facilities not available at nearby pubs such as the Farmers' and the Ivy Bush. The inn stables, were actually 50 yards away along Back Lane — described in 1982 as 'a narrow street of somewhat Dickensian character' — and the entrance to this lane is still via an archway which links the main building to the former brew-house of the inn.

The 'Coachie' remained in the Thomas family until the early 1980s when the last of the line, Miss Imra Thomas, retired. Miss Thomas was a great character who invariably kept the front door of the pub locked — people 'in the know' would use the door in Back Lane. In this way Miss Thomas could regulate who used the inn, and her customers comprised a small circle of friends and regulars. She used to sell nine gallons of beer a week and would take delivery of a nine-gallon firkin once a week from James Williams. When firkins were phased out and replaced by 18-gallon kilderkins, Miss Thomas decided to order one of these every fortnight. 'By the end of the second week the beer was feeling its age', recalled one regular. 'Customers would know to switch from cask beer to bottled beer towards the end of the fortnight'.

The pub, with its marvellously unspoilt interior, was offered for sale by public auction in 1982, the rather lyrical sale particulars noting that the character of the pub had hardly changed 'since Queen Victoria graced the English throne'.

'No longer can home-brewed ale be offered from the keg at 3d. a pint, or a packet of cigarettes at 2d., but the aura of those days lingers on,' wrote the estate agent, adding that in the public bar an original 'Ringers A1 Shag — Get It Here' advertisement remained on display. The pub was purchased by Mr. Nigel Vaughan and underwent the sadly inevitable 'alterations and improvements'. Ken and Mary Green were the licensees for most of the 1990s but the pub closed in 2003 and became a confectionery shop.

Several other pubs may have existed in High Street at various times, including the **Mermaid** which was mentioned in the *Welshman* newspaper in April 1839 as being the venue of a property auction; the **Royal Oak** where Nathaniel Owen was landlord in the 1820s and for which Thomas Llewellyn held the licence in 1835; and the **King's Head** where Griffith James was licensee in 1835. Unfortunately it has proved impossible to discover exactly where these early pubs were located.

CHAPTER TWELVE

Narberth

ST. JAMES STREET, SPRING GARDENS & OUTSKIRTS

St. James Street was once known for part of its length as Sheep Street in recognition of the livestock which was offered for sale here from pens arranged along the pavements. Running north-eastwards from the Market Square, it was the main route into town for anyone arriving from Cardigan or Whitland, but it never really developed the commercial aspect of High Street and boasted far fewer pubs. Instead it seems to have been a street of 'artisan' houses built to accommodate the town's shoemakers and milliners, butchers and ostlers, with one or two rather more imposing residences towards the lower end.

A view of the Butchers' Arms when it was still in operation.

Picture courtesy Narberth Museum.

The **Butchers' Arms,** which stood on the corner of Tabernacle Lane, was opened in 1826 — by a butcher, naturally enough. His name was John Griffiths, and he was still

*The former Butchers' Arms in St. James Street,
as it looked in 2003.*

pouring the pints and carving the joints until his death in the mid 1850s. His widow Martha carried on the business for another ten years, while Thomas Morgan was landlord from 1867 to 1884. David Phillips kept the pub betwen 1891 and 1917 and also brewed his own beer; he was succeeded by Anne Phillips.

The pub was put up for sale in 1922, at which time it comprised 'four excellent rooms on the ground floor, six bedrooms, stabling for 20 horses and a pig-sty'. William Henry Morgan was the landlord from 1923 to 1926 followed by Esther Morgan, who seems to have become Esther Llewellyn the following year. She handed over to M.M. Webb in 1930 and William Owen Davies took over the licence in 1935. In March 1938 the local magistrates turned down a request for the licence to be transferred from Mr. Davies to the owner of the property, Hugh Phillips, and the pub duly closed.

Opposite the Butchers at number nine was a pub called the **Lamb** — an apt name for a Sheep Street ale-house. Thomas Morgan was the landlord in the 1850s; he later moved to run the Butchers' Arms across the road, at which time the Lamb must have closed.

Three doors up from the Lamb was the **Lion** at 12, St. James Street. Sometimes called 'Old Lion', it was opened in the 1860s by a grocer named John Evans, but he died aged 43 in 1872 and the licence passed to his widow Rachel Evans. In 1872 the town magistrates threatened to take away her licence unless she divided up the pub by partitioning off the drinking area from the grocery shop, and a photograph of the pub in the 1890s appears to show a new doorway to the pub, hastily created to the right of the old one. Rachel Evans remarried in 1873, and until 1878 the licensee was her new husband David Williams. He was followed briefly by Nicholas John, while carpenter David Brown kept the Lion from 1880 until the closure of the pub in about 1895.

The pub which still stands on the corner of Spring Gardens and St. James Street began life as the **Gate**, being at one time close to one of the town toll-

*The Lion and the lambs.... This marvellous photograph was taken in the
1890s outside the Old Lion Inn in Sheep Street (now St. James Street).
Note what appears to be an extra doorway inserted at the magistrates'
request to keep the pub part of the premises separate from the shop.*

Picture courtesy of the National Library of Wales.

gates; it seems to have opened in the 1830s. In 1838 the freehold of the inn
was up for sale, the vendors offering:

> All that newly-erected inn called the Gate Inn, most conveniently situated
> for market and fair business. Fitted up with extensive yard and stabling
> and now commanding a profitable business.

John and Elizabeth Howell are recorded as running the Gate between
1836 and 1854 when it passed to Miss Ann Howell. She was still there in
1859, in which year an advert appeared in *Potter's Electric News* offering
for sale by auction 'the public house known by the sign of the Gate Inn',
together with yard and stabling. The name seems to have been changed to
the **Commercial** by the new purchaser, and from 1861 to 1867 the licence
was held by John Phillips, followed in 1871 by his widow Margaret. The

The Kirkland in Narberth in the days when it was still the Commercial.

Picture courtesy of Narberth Museum.

landlord between 1874 and 1891 was Evan Phillips, while David Brown was there in the 1890s.

From 1901 to 1921 the landlord was Frederick Thomas, a noted horse trainer and dealer, who survived an 'alarming fire' in 1907 which destroyed a bedroom. Mr. Thomas appeared at Carmarthen Assizes in 1921 where he was sentenced to 12 months' imprisonment with hard labour for his part in a felony. This conviction disqualified him from ever again holding a public house licence, so it was the name of his wife, Mrs. Irene May Thomas, which appeared over the door between 1921 and her death in 1953. The pub then passed to Gwen Lewis, while Henry Charles Johnston was landlord from 1955 to 1969.

During his time there the pub sign was changed again, to the **Kirkland**, the name deriving from the winning horse in the 1905 Grand National which was trained at Lawrenny. Before setting off for Aintree on the long train journey from Narberth station, Kirkland was apparently stabled overnight at the Commercial Inn. From 1969 to 1983 the 'Kirk' was run in lively fashion by Laurie and Joan Symes who enjoyed organising holiday trips for their regulars, most notably the away fixtures for the darts team against the Spotted Dog pub on the island of Majorca. The pub was also notable for the train set which Mr. Symes — a railway enthusiast — built to run around the back bar. Since 1983 the Kirkland has been kept by Mr. Laurie Edger, the longest-serving licensee in town, and happily the pub has managed to escape any drastic refurbishments and so has retained much of its original character.

A recent view of the 'Kirk'.

Around the corner, opposite the Post Office sorting depot in Spring Gardens was the **Drovers' Arms**. Thomas Williams and his wife Jane seem to have opened the Drovers' in the late 1860s and the pub eventually closed in 1889 when Mr. Williams retired. It became a private house and was later divided into two properties, 29 and 29a Spring Gardens.

Across the road, the **Farmers' Arms** on the corner of Spring Gardens and Plaindealings (now Northfield) Road also opened in the late 1860s. A gardener named John Williams was the first licensee and he ran the pub until 1884, by which time he was nearly 70. Evan Phillips held the licence from 1889 until his death in 1896 when his widow Sophia took over.

Walter Williams was the landlord from 1900 to 1906 while from 1907 to 1927 the licence was held by the wine merchants firm of James Williams who presumably installed managers to run the business. Mrs. Mary Lewis took over in 1928 and she was still there in 1955, being helped by her sons Royce and Terry. Jack Hallwood then took up the tenancy of this James Williams house and he opened up the cellars for the purpose of storing the casks of beer. The beer was then drawn up to the bar by pump — reputedly the first time this arrangement had been seen in Narberth where it was the practice to serve beer straight from a barrel behind the bar. Mr. Hallwood left in 1964, and the Farmers' was subsequently run for over 15 years by Walter Mullens. At one time very popular with farmers and auctioneers on mart day, the Farmers' has changed hands

149

The Farmers' Arms as it appeared in 2001.

several times in recent years. It was altered internally a few years ago as part of the trend for 'open plan' bars.

A few doors up was the **Salutation** at 6, Northfield Road, where the landlord from 1871 to 1875 was James Davies; in October 1877 the licence passed from him to a blacksmith named John James. In 1880, a Gypsy called Anne Lovell was sent to jail for 14 days after being found guilty of pretending to tell fortunes in the Salutation. She told the landlord's daughter, Emily, 'You are a very lucky young woman and will have many sweethearts' and relieved her of a silver shilling for the information. John James remained licensee until the closure of the pub in 1895; the smithy next door (now 6a) continued to flourish into the 1920s.

The **Plaindealings Arms** was a small pub on the outskirts of Narberth which had no accommodation for lodgers and stabling for only three horses. It was on the right hand side of Northfield Road, about 300 yards from the Farmers' Arms and just past Bloomfield. Owned by the Lewis Lloyd family, the Plaindealings Arms was kept by butter-merchant David Williams and his wife Esther from 1861 to 1871; in 1869 they were robbed of beef and beer by a thief who broke in while they were at chapel. John and Hannah Henton were licensees from 1873 to 1891, Hannah later running the pub on her own until the turn of the century.

The Plaindealings in retirement.

Mrs. Ann John held the licence from 1904 to 1914. Henry John then took over and he was still there when the pub lost its licence in 1918 under the redundancy regulations. Owner of the premises Miss L.B. Lewis Lloyd received compensation of £236; Henry John pocketed £26.

The railway reached Narberth in 1866, although the station was slightly out of town on the road to Crinow. A small hotel was built opposite the station for the convenience of travellers, and John Lewis kept the grandly named **Royal Hotel** in 1868. However, since everyone called it the **Station Hotel**, this soon became the official name. The hotel was the property of William Davies of Swansea, an agent of the Burton Brewery Company, and for much of his tenancy, John Lewis duly obtained his supplies from Burton Brewery. In 1872, however, he decided to switch to selling Alsopp's beer, the predictable consequence being that the irate owner gave him notice to quit. Lewis left and the licence passed to George Harries who was still the land-lord in 1875.

Lewis had the last laugh, however, because by 1876 he was back at the Station Hotel, having purchased the business. He died in 1882, but his widow Mrs. Maria Lewis carried on running the hotel. The last licensee appears to have been Theophilus Thomas who was there in 1891, after which the inn was run for a number of years as a temperance hotel. It was the last building in the terrace on the left leading down to the station.

Ben John — 'Ben the Bus' — outside the Station Hotel in 1938.
Picture courtesy of Narberth Museum.

When John Lewis was booted out of the Station Hotel in 1872, he responded by building a red brick shack on a bank near the station and applying for a licence. This was granted in 1873 (despite fierce opposition from the owner of the Station Hotel) and by 1874 Lewis was happily running a rival station pub which he called the **Locomotive**. Even after he returned to the Station Hotel he carried on running the Locomotive as well, as did his widow Maria in later years. However the Locomotive closed in 1884 when the magistrates chose not to renew the licence and the whereabouts of the old pub cannot now be determined.

The **Union Tavern** was a hillside inn to the south of Narberth on the turnpike road to Cold Blow. It was kept by Rees Protheroe from 1822 to 1835, while Mary Protheroe was the landlady in 1841. It seems to have closed shortly afterwards and must have been located near the quarry which nowaday is home to a tool and plant hire concern.

Just below the Union Tavern was a property known as Providence, the home of a long line of butchers called Williams. The closure of the Union Tavern seems to have encouraged them to open it as a pub, the **Providence** inn, and it was run in the 1850s by John Williams. He died in 1861 and George Williams, another butcher, was next in line, followed by his daughter Ada Williams who married Nicholas John. They kept the pub for a few years before handing over to John Thomas in 1873. When Mr. Thomas moved to the Eagle in 1877, the Providence passed to another local butcher named Thomas Eynon.

The Providence is now a private house.

The building was repaired and re-roofed in 1880 at a cost of £185, and in August 1882 it was offered for sale by auction, together with brewhouse, outbuildings and fields. By this time the licence had passed from Thomas Eynon (senior) to Thomas Eynon (junior). Howell James took over in 1883, while a tailor named James Williams held the licence in 1891 and Daniel Bibby was there in 1895. William Bevan was the licensee from 1896 to 1911, the licence being transferred in November of that year to Thomas R. Evans who remained the landlord until his death in 1938. It was reported in February 1939 that the Providence had been sold and that the new owners were converting it into a house.

In the early 1860s, David Gibby and his wife Mary moved from the Welcome to Town in High Street to open the **Cresselly Arms** near Narberth bridge — possibly at 3, Bridge Hill. The pub was soon in trouble with the law and in 1865 the town magistrates refused to renew the licence 'in consequence of this house not having been conducted in a satisfactory manner'. By 1881, Gibby was earning a living as a horse jockey, despite being in his 60s.

Two town pubs have proved impossible to pin down. William Phillip is recorded as being the landlord of the **Boar's Head**, Narberth, in 1784, while a pub of the same name somewhere in Narberth was kept by Benjamin Rogers between 1827 and 1835. Also one of the town's various **New Inns** was kept by Thomas Eynon and Thomas Llewellin in the 1820s, but no information as to its whereabouts has come to light.

MEASURED from HYDE PARK CORNER	From Milford	LONDON to BATH AND BRISTOL, CONTINUED TO HAVERFORDWEST AND MILFORD.	From London	THROUGH CALNE and CHIPPENHAM.
lightful pleasure grounds, from many parts of which a beautiful prospect of the surrounding country is obtained.—— St. Helens, Capt. *Jones*; Marino, *J. H. Vivian*, Esq.; Lower Sketty, Capt. *C. Ward*; Sketty Park, Sir *J. Morris*, Bart.; and Sketty Hall, *C. Baring*, Esq. This charming villa is situated on an eminence, and enjoys many fine views, including the whole of Swansea Bay, and Oystermouth Castle, the ruins of which magnificent fortress occupy a gentle eminence, and command a delightful prospect of the surrounding country; many parts of the buildingare in good preservation, and the grand gateway is nearly perfect.	55¾	Brymind	217½	NEATH, near, on an eminence, Gnoll Castle, *H. Grant*, Esq. This noble castellated mansion stands on the summit of a hill, at the termination of a fine lawn; it commands many delightful views, and is encompassed by hanging woods, shady walks, extensive plantations, and beautifully picturesque cascades.—— Near this is Courtherbert, *W. Gronow*, Esq.; and farther to the right, Dyffryn, Mrs. *Williams*; 4½ m. distant from Neath, Killybebill, Mrs. *Bassett*; and 2 m. beyond Neath, Gelligron, *Owen Rees*, Esq.; Drumma House, *John Fenton*, Esq.; and Glanbrane, Major *William Jones*; 4 m. beyond Neath, Gwernllwynwith, *C. H. Smith*, Esq.; and Birchgrove, Mrs. *Morgan Morgan*.
	53¼	* Llannan	220	
	49¾	Pontyberem	223½	
	45¾	Llangyndeyrn	227½	
		3 m. farther.		
		to Llanelly 11 m.		
	40½	* *CAERMARTHEN,* Ivy Bush	232¾	
		To Llandilo Vaur 14½ m. / To Llanbeder 23½ m.		CROSS INON. Penllergaer, *L. W. Dillwyn*, Esq.; and Brynwhilac,——.
		to Kidwely 9 m.		
CAERMARTHEN, entrance of, Iron and Tin Mills belonging to Messrs. *Reynolds & Smith*; 1 m. distant, Peterwell, Rev. *D. Peter*; Myrtle Hill, *J. Davies*, Esq.; Ystrad Lodge, *J. Jones*, Esq.; and Rhyd y gorse, *D. J. Edwardes*, Esq.; 4 m. distant, Towey Castle, Rev. *W. Evans*; Upland, Miss *Thomas*; and Cappel Dewi,— *Morris*, Esqrs.; 5 m. distant, Sarnau, *R. Waters*, Esq.; and Clogddu, *J. Davies*, Esq.; on the east bank of the river Towey, Iscoed, Rev. *E. Picton*; about 6 m. from Caermarthen, Llwyndu, Capt. *Hardinge*; Gelly-dêg, *R. T. Dixie*, Esq.; and Pilrhoath, *W. B. Gwyn*, Esq.; 8 miles from Caermarthen, Llanstephan, *George Meares*, Esq.	39	Stony Bridge	234½	GIBRANLWY, near, Forest Hall,——.
	31	* St. Clare's Bridge	242½	CAERMARTHEN. ¼ mile distant, Job's Well, Major *Nott*; and Sterling Park, Mrs. *Stephenson*; Fountain Hall, *J. Griffiths*, Esq.; and Lime Grove, *S. Morris*, Esq.; beyond which is Llwntêg, *C. Morgan*, Esq.; and Bwlch, *T. Beynon*, Esq.
		To Haverfordwest, through Whitland, 21½m.		
		Cross the river Taff		
		to Llaugharn 3 m.		
		London to LLAUGHARN 245¾ m.		
	29	Llandowror	244½	LLAUGHARN is situated at the mouth of the river Towey, where, on a low rock, stand the remains of its ancient castle, which is said to have been destroyed by Llewellyn, Prince of North Wales. A small market is held in this town on Saturday.
		* *Tavernspite,*		
	24	*Pembrokeshire*	249½	
	21	Princes Gate	252½	
		to Ludchurch ¼ m.		
NARBERTH. This neat little town is pleasantly situated on an eminence, in a narrow vale, and chiefly derives support from its contiguity to the great western road, along which the mail passes and re-passes daily. The privilege of holding a market on Thursday was granted to this place in the reign of James II. Here was formerly a spacious and well-fortified castle, but few of its remains are now in existence; yet these have a fine picturesque appearance, and afford some idea of its original consequence.	20	Cold Blow	253½	LLAUGHARN. Llaugharn Castle, Col. *Starke*.
		to Templeton 1 m., thence to Tenby 6½ m. to Pembroke 12½ m.		
	18½	* *NARBERTH*	255	ROBBESTON WATHEN. Rev. *James James*.
	16½	Robbeston Wathen	256¾	
		To St. Clare's Bridge 11 m.		
	15½	to Caniston Bridge	257¾	CANISTON BRIDGE, ¼ m. distant, Ridgway, Mrs. *Foley*. This charming residence is surrounded by delightful groves, it commands a fine prospect of the woods of Caniston, Slebech, &c., and from the lawn, a good view of the ruins of Llanhauaden Castle presents itself.
		Cross the river Olethy		
MID-COUNTY HOUSE, 1 m. beyond, Picton Castle, *R. Bulkeley Phillips*, Esq. This noble edifice was erected about the time of William Rufus; it is remarkable as having always been occupied, and still retains its embattled figure, notwithstanding the various alterations and additions of successive inhabitants. The extensive grounds are judiciously laid out, and, besides being richly wooded, contain every advantageof water-scenery from the approximation of two noble streams which flow into Milford Haven.—— Near this is Slebech Hall, the elegant mansion of *E. Phillips*, Esq.	12¾	Mid-County House	260½	MID-COUNTY HOUSE, beyond, at Wiston, Wiston Castle, Lord *Cawdor*. The present noble mansion is said to include some of the walls of the ancient castle, which was an extensive and very strong building, but now totally in ruins, with the exception of part of the keep.
		Before Haverfordwest,		
		To Cardigan 26¼ m. / To Fishguard 14 m., thence to Newport 6m.		
		Cross the river Hiog		
	7½	* *HAVERFORD-WEST*	265¾	
		To St. David's 15¾ m.		
MAWDLEN'S BRIDGE, 2m. distant, Fern Hill, Sir *H. Matthias*; beyond which is Boulston,	6½	Mawdlen's Bridge	266¾	STAINTON. Thornton, Mrs. *Crimes*; at Roberston, Robeston Hall, *W. H. Scourfield*, Esq.; farther to the right, Rosepool,
		To Tier's Cross 4 m., thence to Hubberston 3¼ m., thence to Hakin, on Milford Haven, 1 m.		

The route through Narberth from Paterson's Roads *of 1829.*

CHAPTER THIRTEEN

Llanddewi Velfrey to Llawhaden

Llanddewi Velfrey is a small roadside village which nowadays takes its name from the church dedicated to St. David on the hillside to the south. There may have been a settlement near the church at one time, but the present hill-top community developed in the late 18th and early 19th centuries when the ridgeway road west of Whitland was 'turnpiked'. Several ale-houses were established here to provide refreshments for travellers who had made the tiring ascent from the valleys below, and by 1795 Thomas David, David Prout and Edward Edwards were among those running ale-houses alongside the turnpike road.

Approaching from the Whitland direction, the first ale-house to be encountered would have been the **Wheelabout** on the north side of the road. According to local tradition the Wheelabout was the site of the last cock-pit in Wales, but for this to be true the cock-pit must have survived long after the

The former Wheelabout inn at Llanddewi Velfrey.

155

pub itself had closed. In 1772 the Wheelabout was occupied by Rees Lewis and when the freehold of this 'well-accustomed inn' was advertised as being for sale in April 1820 the tenant was Thomas Lewis. It seems to have closed as an inn shortly after the sale and become a farm; the property is now known as 'Glenfield'.

A hundred yards further west, on the opposite side of the road, was **Cross Inn**. There's no crossroads here now, but at one time a well-used trackway crossed the ridgeway at this point, linking the farms in the Taf Vale to the north with those in the Lampeter Vale to the south. William Lewis lived at Cross Inn from 1841 to 1871, although whether it was still an inn at this stage is difficult to determine. The cottage is still called Cross Inn and it stands pine-end on to the present main road, facing onto the almost vanished north-south trackway which is now little more than a footpath.

Although the village is now called Llanddewi Velfrey, it originally took its name from the local pub — a fairly common practice. Unfortunately for the new settlement, however, the ale-house had the decidedly mundane name of **Commercial**. The Commercial was a busy crossroads pub, where licensee Nathaniel Scourfield hosted a gathering of the Tithe Commissioners in 1839 and a meet of the Begelly hounds in 1843. Mr. Scourfield gave up the pub in

The Parcylan in Llanddewi Velfrey in about 1908.

Picture courtesy of Mr. Roger Davies.

the 1850s in rather contentious circumstances; it is said that the irascible landlord had his licence taken away after arguing with the squire of Henllan and pouring a jug of beer over him! In later years the Commercial became a shop and village post office.

When the Commercial closed, the licence was transferred to another building on Commercial Cross. Blacksmith William Stephens opened the **Parcylan** in the 1850s and he ran it until his death in 1898 when his widow Frances took over. It was probably a typical cottage ale-house to begin with, but was substantially enlarged at a later stage. William Thomas took over the Parcylan in 1901 and ran it for half a century, brewing his own beer in a shed next to the pub and delivering it by horse and cart to outlying farms. When brewing ceased at the pub in the 1920s the horse and cart were used to collect barrels of beer from Llanfallteg station. Following Mr. Thomas' death at the age of 86 in 1953, the business was carried on by his daughter Theodosia Thomas until 1977. James Evans took over, followed by Roger and Ann Davies and then Noel Corrigan who ran the pub in the early 1990s before moving to re-open the Alpha in Tavernspite. He was followed for five years by 'Geordie' Fraser, who now runs the Boar's Head in Templeton, since when there have been several different tenants of this attractive Felinfoel-owned pub.

*A recent view of the Parcylan — a rare case of
a Pembrokeshire pub with a Welsh name.*

157

There were a couple of other ale-houses in and around the village. Henry Hall was the landlord of the **Plough and Harrow** in 1822-24, while Stepin Farm on the 'old road' to Henllan was probably the **Step In** pub at some stage in the dim and distant past.

West of Llanddewi Velfrey was an ale-house which — like the Parcylan — had a Welsh name. This was **Ffynnongwelluabach** where William Beynon was the landlord from 1822 to 1826. The name, which occurs in several different spellings, can be translated as 'well which is more fruitful than a cow', and it was the presence of this spring of fresh water which persuaded the baptists to build Ffynnon chapel here in 1723. The inn appears to have been in existence before the chapel — a manslaughter incident took place at an ale-house near Ffynnon in 1670 — and the local baptists are thought to have held regular prayer meetings at the inn before their chapel was built. In those early days, the battle lines had not been drawn up between nonconformity and the demon drink, but as time passed the chapel and ale-house must have become uneasy neighbours and by 1841 the Beynon family was farming at Ffynnon with no hint that beer was still being brewed and sold on the premises.

Penblewyn Cross, where the Narberth to Cardigan road crossed the Whitland turnpike, was a prime position for an ale-house and in 1841 farmer and publican David Phillips ran the **Royal Exchange** on the crossroads. This was an important gathering point for the drovers, and it is said that the cattle would be penned overnight at nearby Parc-yr-efail before being shod for the long journey east. By 1851 the name of the ale-house had been changed to the **Speculation**, but it was more commonly known as 'Gibby's', because

This old farm building at Penblewyn is thought to have been the Royal Exchange and later the Speculation.

from the 1840s to 1863 the inn was tenanted by Thomas Gibby who also farmed 25 acres of land nearby. Freehold of the inn-cum-farm changed hands at auction in the summer of 1863 and by 1867 the licensee was Thomas Thomas. The inn, which closed shortly afterwards, is thought to have occupied the old farmhouse building fronting onto the roundabout, the present Penblewyn farmhouse being of more recent construction.

Moving further west, the **Bridge** at Coxlake has also been known in its day as the **Bridge End** inn and — mercifully briefly — the **Dick Turpin**. This may have been the beer-house run by William Scourfield, victualler and blacksmith of Robeston Wathen, who was imprisoned for debt in 1838. (He drank himself to death two years later). Mary Smith kept the Bridge at Coxlake in 1841 and a widow named Elizabeth John was there in 1851. When landlord George Price died in 1869 the licence passed to Elizabeth Price and she was still pouring the pints, aged 82, in 1883. Samuel Thomas kept the pub in the 1890s followed by John and Mary Ann Harkett and then Sidney and Elizabeth Davies.

The landlord from 1914 to 1932 was Thomas Skyrme, the licence passing to Mrs. Charlotte Skyrme who remained until 1939. John Billinghurst was licensee during the war, after which the pub was bought by William Grey. In 1953, an advertisement stated: 'The whole of the property has recently been completely renovated or rebuilt and is now one of the most modern licensed premises in the county'. Even so, when the Bridge was taken over by Gerwyn Owen and his wife Nancy in 1959 it was described as being 'no more than a small country pub, able to hold at the most a dozen people'. The Owens greatly extended the premises by building two lounges

The frontage of the Bridge Inn, Robeston Wathen, in 2002.

159

The function room of the Bridge Inn, shortly after it had been opened in the 1960s.

Picture courtesy of Mr. Stephen Evans.

and a function room complete with Hammond organ. In the 1960s the pub boasted a resident organist, and coach parties would travel from all over Pembrokeshire to enjoy the music and dancing in 'the plush surroundings and homely atmosphere' of the Bridge. The Owens were the first to organise regular talent competitions in the county, which proved very popular, and they also developed a caravan site in the valley beyond the pub. They ran the Bridge for some 20 years, and it was later owned for a time by Mr. Nigel Vaughan who engaged managers to run it as part of his chain of 'Vaughany Inns'. With the recent arrival of new proprietor Stephen Evans the Bridge has come full circle in some ways, since he is a relative of the Skyrme family which ran the pub many years earlier. Also his father Eifion Evans — sometime mine host at the Angel in Narberth — was the Bridge Inn's regular organist during the heady days of Gerwyn Owen. Mr. Evans has recently refurbished the bar and function room and the pub — one of the first in Pembrokeshire to operate a 'smoke free' policy — has an interesting collection of old photographs of the area.

In one of these photographs can be glimpsed the **Coach and Horses** in Robeston Wathen village, which was once an inn where stage-coaches would halt to change horses. In 1820, Thomas Roscoe stopped at the inn and described it in his *Wanderings and Excursions in South Wales*: 'For a roadside hostelrie I found in it more appliances of comfort than I expected and mine host was active in his civilities'. The actively civil landlord was almost certainly Thomas Llewhellin who was still there in 1844.

From 1846 to 1852 the landlord was Thomas Smith, who described himself as 'brewer, publican and dealer in beer, spirits, tobacco and tea'. (He appears to have been the husband of Mary Smith who kept the Bridge in 1841). From 1858 to 1861 the landlord was Scotsman Thomas Muir, and from 1867 to 1875 it was publican and gardener Morgan Lewis. James Llewellyn was there from 1878 to 1887, when it was the registered office of a Friendly Society called the True Britons' Society, but by 1891 it had become a farm known as the 'Old Coach and Horses'. It is now a private property, Penfidir House.

When the Greyhound moved in the 1870s it was to this cottage near Canaston Bridge.

The **Greyhound**, which was originally located in the centre of Robeston Wathen, was first mentioned in 1845 and may have taken its name from one of the stage-coaches which regularly halted in the hill-top village. It was kept by farmer James Peters from 1851 to 1861 and by Thomas Webb and his sister Mary from 1867 to 1871. In September 1873, the licence of the Greyhound was moved from the original house to a new location outside the village, both properties being owned by Manorbier mason George Saunders.

There is a reference to a publican called John Evans in the 1841 census, and it appears that his inn was just outside Robeston Wathen. A note on the census describes the property as 'Rest', so it seems likely that this short-lived pub was called the **Travellers' Rest**.

Now much modernised and extended, the **Bush,** on the way down to Canaston Bridge, was once a tiny hillside cottage inn which only had one external door until 1910. In that year the magistrates at Narberth grudgingly gave licensee James Freeman permission to fit a back door to the pub as a convenience for himself and his family. 'It must not be used for any other purpose,' warned the magistrates sternly, obviously having in mind out-of-hours drinking sessions.

The Bush dates from at least the early 1840s and was run in the late 1840s by James Thomas, formerly a coachman with the Rev. J.W. James of Robeston Wathen. The railway was being driven through countryside to the north of Narberth at this time, and Thomas decided to earn a few extra shillings as a

The Bush, a much-altered hillside inn outside Robeston Wathen.

labourer. He was helping to dig out the deep cutting at Egremont when one of the walls of the cutting collapsed, killing him instantly. He left a young widow and four children, the widow Mary Thomas continuing to run the pub until the early 1890s. Mary Williams succeeded her, but David Thomas kept the pub and farmed the land around between 1900 and 1906, followed by the afore-mentioned James Freeman. The pub was closed for a time in 1917 as tenant Thomas Samuel fell foul of DORA — the stringent wartime licensing laws introduced under the Defence of the Realm Act.

The Bush was eventually re-opened by Benjamin Mathias who remained in charge until 1921, while Charlie Thomas was the landlord from 1923 to 1929 before he moved to the Milford Arms in Haverfordwest. (Somewhat surprisingly, the owner of the pub at this time was Lady Chatfield, her husband Admiral Sir Alfred Montacute Chatfield being the son of a former superintendent of Pembroke Dockyard). Benjie Mathias again took over the running of the pub in the early 1930s, followed in 1935 by his widow Ellen. When she moved to the Ivy Bush in Narberth in 1940, Matthew Jones took charge for the next ten years. The Bush was then purchased by the well-remembered Idris Griffiths — 'Idris the Bush' — who remained the licensee until 1977 after which it changed hands several times. Since about 1990 the Bush has been owned by Greyhawk Leisure of Monmouthshire which has engaged various managers to run the business.

162

When the **Greyhound** moved it was to a building on the same side of the road as the Bush but much further down the hill. George Saunders, the chap responsible for the move, ran the pub until his death in 1884 after which Ellen Saunders became the licensee. A joiner named Lewis Morgan, was there from 1891 to 1906, in which year the pub closed. Now called 'Ben-y-Mar', it was the lower of the two roadside cottages near the foot of the hill.

Canaston Bridge has always been an important link between the south-east of the county and the rest of Pembrokeshire, being for many years the lowest bridging point on the Eastern Cleddau; in the 1840s a coracle was kept on standby at a nearby house to transport pedestrians whenever the Cleddau burst its banks and flooded the road! Rowland Bateman ran an ale-house near here in 1784, as did Elizabeth Bateman in 1795, but where this was isn't recorded. Somewhat surprisingly there doesn't seem to have been another ale-house at this point for many years afterwards. However, the records of the Narberth Petty Sessions for February 1874 contain the following entry:

> It is ordered that the licence of the **Cannaston Bridge** [*sic*] in the parish
> of Robeston Wathen, lately held by Stephen Prickett deceased, be trans-
> ferred to James Prickett, son of the present tenant of the premises.

Obviously young James, who was a blacksmith by trade, wasn't cut out to be a publican because he didn't bother to renew the licence at the brewster sessions the following September.

There was an ale-house licence issued in respect of Blackpool Mill between 1795 and 1828, presumably so that workmen at the mill and the nearby iron-foundry could obtain liquid refreshment 'on site', the nearest alehouse being some distance away.

The medieval village of Llawhaden is notable for its fine castle, one of the residences of the bishops of St. David's. It has never been well served for pubs, however, although there was an ale-house called the **Royal Oak** somewhere in the village which William Howell kept in 1824-25. There is also a local

The former New Inn at Llawhaden.

tradition that the Red House near Llawhaden Church was once an ale-house called the **Bridge**.

Near the castle entrance was the **New Inn** where William Reed was landlord from 1784 to 1822 and Mary Reed was landlady from 1823 to 1828. This was the registered office of the Llawhaden Castle Friendly Society, which was established in 1843, and also the meeting place of the Manorial Court for the Baronry and Townreed of Llawhaden. William Thomas was the landlord in 1841, but in 1851 the inn was being run by his widow Jane Thomas who shared the house with her elderly uncle, Joseph Reed, and her 25-year-old nephew, Joseph Reed Williams. Old Joseph, who had been brewer to Lord Milford at Picton Castle for much of his life, died in March 1853 at the age of 92. The New Inn seems to have been taken over later that year by William Price, while Thomas Williams of Wiston was landlord from 1861 to 1871, running the pub with the help of his wife Jane and also farming eight acres. When the New Inn closed isn't known, but it doesn't appear as a pub on the 1881 census.

This building in a fork of the road near Bethesda was once the Mill Inn.

When Joseph Reed Williams left the New Inn in 1853 it was to run the **Mill Inn** at Pont Shan and farm about 130 acres of land around. This inn must have had some connection with Pont Shan corn mill which stood about a mile north of Redstone Cross and where members of the Williams family were millers at one time. The Mill Inn itself occupied a triangle of ground where the road forked, one branch leading to Bethesda, the other to Llawhaden. A son of Henry and Mary Williams who ran the Cambrian inn at Pembroke Dock, Joseph Reed Williams remained at the Mill Inn for over 30 years. Martha Williams, his widow, was licensee from 1891 until her death in 1898, after which the pub was run for couple of years by their son, David Williams. Mr. W.B. Harries took over in 1903, while from 1904 to 1909 the landlady was Mrs. Eliza Harries. The pub closed the following year.

Just up the road, the village of Bethesda had an ale-house in the 1820s kept by Ann Wilkins. The 1891 census mentions a house called **Cross Inn**, Bethesda Cross, which was presumably the former ale-house, but otherwise nothing is known about it.

CHAPTER FOURTEEN

Clunderwen and Llandysilio

Above Penblewyn Cross, the main road north of Narberth climbs steadily to cross the high ridge of the Preseli Hills before dropping down into Cardigan. This has long been an important trade route, and, naturally, numerous ale-houses sprang up along the way to provide rest and refreshment for travellers and their horses. A mile or so north of Penblewyn is Grondre, now a small and scattered community which has been rather overshadowed in the last 150 years by the development of Clunderwen to the north. However, in the early 19th century much of the traffic heading north from Narberth market or Ludchurch quarries would have passed over Longford Bridge at Grondre before taking the left hand fork towards Maenclochog or the right hand fork towards Efailwen. This horse-drawn traffic bottleneck was an ideal place for an ale-house, and Grondre seems to have had three of them at various times. One of these was the **Boar's Head** which was run by the Morgan family. In 1812 John Morgan held an ale-house licence for a house at Grondre which was probably the Boar's Head, while the landlord in the 1820s was David Morgan. Its exact position is unknown.

It is said that carters transporting lime from Ludchurch to the Maenclochog area would break their journey at Grondre, resting the horses overnight before completing the long uphill haul the following day. This gave rise to the name of the ale-house and smallholding still known as **Weary Team** where Mary Thomas was the licensee in 1841. When it stopped being an ale-house isn't recorded, but it is believed that cart-horses were still stabled there for many years afterwards while the drivers headed for the ale-house diagonally across the road.

This was the **Square and Compass** where John Owen was the landlord in 1841. Evan James was running the pub and farming 14 acres in 1851, while the landlord between 1858 and 1895 was David Davies. His son-in-law Stephen Griffiths — a coachman by trade — was the landlord from 1901 to 1917 when the licence was withdrawn under the redundancy ruling. A thatched cottage pub, with stabling on the premises for just one horse, the Square and Compass did little trade in its latter days and the landlord was probably glad to receive the compensation when it closed. Weary Team and the Square and Compass are now private houses, much renovated and pleasantly by-passed following a major re-alignment of the main road a few years ago.

The Square and Compass stopped selling beer in 1917.

Further northwards, alongside the main road, stood the **Wheatensheaf** which was kept in 1841 by 30-year-old John James. By 1851 the name had apparently changed to the **Farmers' Arms,** with Martha James as licensee, but it was back to Wheatensheaf by 1858 when stonemason and innkeeper David Peregrine was in charge. Griff Davies, butcher, was living at the Wheatensheaf in 1871, by which time it no longer seems to have been a pub.

On a cold December day in 1853, crowds gathered to witness an unusual launching ceremony not far from the Wheatensheaf. As onlookers cheered and workmen waved their hats in the air, Miss Protheroe of Dolwilym House, Llanglydwen smashed a bottle of wine against the metal walls of a newly-built station hotel and declared it open.

It was in 1852 that the South Wales Railway reached the borders of Pembrokeshire, passing under the main Narberth to Cardigan turnpike road two miles north of Penblewyn. At the time this was the closest the railway came to the fashionable resort of Tenby, so this fairly isolated farming community suddenly found itself with a station which was an important link in the west Wales transport network. Captain William Protheroe of nearby Dolwilym House recognised that an hotel was urgently required at Narberth Road (as the new station was called) but rather than build one in the conventional way out of bricks and mortar, he decided to order one 'off the peg' from a firm in Bristol which specialised in prefabricated iron buildings. Shortly afterwards a goods train arrived at Narberth Road containing various lengths of timber, together with doors and windows and an enormous amount of corrugated iron sheeting. 'Within the short space of three weeks', marvelled the correspondent from the *Welshman* newspaper, 'a most commodious hotel has been erected'.

Iron Duke advertisements:
Top : 1881. Bottom : 1937.

The iron pub was named the **Iron Duke** in honour of the Duke of Wellington, who had died the previous year, and after Miss Protheroe had performed the naming ceremony 'the workmen and others were beautifully regaled with a substantial dinner' in the new building. There must have been another celebration at the inn a few weeks later, because the station at Narberth Road was officially opened on 2 January, 1854. The first licensees of the Iron Duke appear to have been William and Harriet Smith — Harriet running the place on her own following her husband's death at the early age of 46 in 1863. By the 1870s, Narberth Road had grown into a fair-sized railway village — re-named Clunderwen after a local manor house — and the Iron Duke was said to command a large business and was 'a good posting house'. Harriet Smith retired in the late 1870s to run a pastry shop in the village and the proprietor in 1881 was John Williams from Milford Haven.

Disaster struck the Iron Duke on a November night in 1889. A beam running alongside one of the chimney flues ignited and soon the building was on fire. As the *Welshman* reported:

> As there was a good deal of wood used in the construction of the hotel, the whole building was quickly enveloped in flames and was reduced to ashes in a very short time. Fortunately no lives were lost, but nothing of much value was saved.

The landlord at the time was a clog-maker named William Freshney, and it was reported that not only had he lost all his furniture, but all his family's clothing had been destroyed in the blaze. A collection was organised in the village to help the family, the Iron Duke was rebuilt as a four-square building of conventional construction, and Mr. Freshney carried on as licensee until about 1895.

Mrs. Phoebe Thomas was running the Iron Duke by the turn of the century and she was still there well into the 1920s, while the new proprietor in 1937

Clunderwen was a busy railway junction when this photograph, showing the Iron Duke, was taken in the early 20th century.

was Mr. A.J. Thomas. It was a very busy pub at this time, especially as the regular cattle mart was located close by and the station was still fully operational. Subsequent licensees included Theo Thomas and his brother John — 'John the Duke'. In December 1961 the Iron Duke was sold at a public auction on the premises, being bought for £6,500 by Haverfordwest businessman Emlyn Bonnell of the Harford Café in Quay Street. It was during Mr. Bonnell's time at the pub that the railway network suffered drastic cutbacks, and the attractive station buildings opposite the Iron Duke were sadly demolished. The approach to the pub was also changed at about this time, with one of the old station sidings being replaced by a tarmac road. A Yorkshireman, Richard 'Dickie' Wright ran the Iron Duke during the 1980s, after which there were several changes of licensee before the present landlord, Mr Simon Fussell, took over in the mid 1990s.

Until about five years ago the **Narberth Arms** — or 'The Nackie' as it was always known — stood opposite the road down to Clunderwen station. The early history of this hostelry is a little vague, but it may have been the place known as the **Railway Hotel** which was run by Hugh Phillipps at the time of the 1861 census. John Lewis was landlord of the Narberth Arms, Narberth Road according to a trade directory of 1867, while John and Hester Williams

The Iron Duke as it looked in 2003.

were there from 1879 to 1881. A widow named Mrs. Rachel Davies was land-lady from 1891 until her death in 1906; she brewed and sold her own beer with the help of her daughter Sarah, who was also a widow. It is said that in 1904 the first meeting of the local farmers' co-operative movement was held in the loft above the stables of the pub. Morris Davies was landlord in 1914 and John Morris was there in the 1920s. Best remembered of the Narberth Arms licensees were David and Mabel Lewis who ran this James Williams house from the 1960s to the early '80s, while among the recent landlords was former television actor Ronnie Williams — one half of the Welsh comedy duo Ryan and Ronnie. The closure of the Narberth Arms a few years ago left the Iron Duke as the only pub in the village.

Just up the road on the right was the **Tafarn Newydd**, a large but fairly short-lived pub which began life as Raffles Nite-spot in the 1980s. It was converted into a pub by Denis and Joan Saunderson in 1989 and was later taken over by James Williams, but closed soon afterwards.

When stonemason David Peregrine left the Wheatensheaf in the 1860s, it was to open a new ale-house nearby which he called the **Masons' Arms.** This stood at the bottom end of Masons Row (the name of which lives on) and it may be that Mr. Peregrine built the terrace which included the locally famous

An early view of the Narberth Arms in Clunderwen.
Picture courtesy of Roger Davies.

Clunderwen 'emporium'. He was still the licensee of the pub in 1881, while Rees Edwards was there from 1891 to 1895 and Thomas and Elizabeth Owen were the licensees in 1901. Benjamin Phillips was running the Masons' Arms in 1906 and he was followed by Mrs. E. Phillips, who was licensee in 1914. The pub was closed under the compensation ruling in 1922, when it too was a James Williams house, and it later became a butcher's shop. It is now a private house.

A couple of miles further north, the village of Llandysilio straddles the main road. Various country lanes and trackways converge at this point, and this meeting of the ways prompted the development of a fair-sized village during the early and middle parts of the 19th century. Several ale-houses were estab-

The Mason's Arms is on the right of this early view of Clunderwen.
Picture courtesy of Mr. Ken Daniels.

170

lished in the village (despite a strong noncon-formist presence) and two of them are still open today.

The **Pwllcwarre Arms** isn't numbered among the survivors, although the building still stands. This may be the pub that appears as 'Quarrow, Llandissilio' in the 1822 list of ale-house recognisances when the landlady was Ann Griffiths. The Griffiths family continued to live at Pwllcwarre for much of the 19th century, the house being alongside the large quarry from which it derived its name. Saddler Thomas James and his wife Emma were the licensees in 1881, and when Mr. James died at the age of 52 in 1890, Mrs. James took over. She

The Masons' Arms is now a private house.

The former Pwllcwarre Arms next to the village post office in Llandysilio.

carried on running the pub until 1901 and her son Percy James was the land-lord in 1906. The pub, which was in the building adjoining the present Llandysilio post office, seems to have closed by the First World War. Also in this area was the short-lived **Fountain Inn** where James Howells was landlord in 1861.

On the left hand side heading north was the **Saddlers' Arms** on the corner near Pisgah chapel. Thomas James — 'James the Saddler' — was the landlord from 1871 to 1875 before moving to run the Pwllcwarre Arms, while Rachael Davies was the landlady in 1881 before she moved even further down the road, to the Narberth Arms in Clunderwen. She was followed by Mrs. Phoebe Evans, a lady who was widowed at an early age. She ran the pub and brewed her own beer for nearly 20 years, while her son Griff Evans built and ran the drapery shop next door known as Manchester House. By 1906 John Thomas was the

The Evans family pictured outside their various business concerns in Llandysilio in about 1905. Griff Evans ran a drapery business at Manchester House, while his mother Phoebe (standing below the 'S' of Saddlers) was the licensee of the Saddlers' Arms for many years.

Picture courtesy of Linda Atherton.

landlord of the Saddlers' Arms, while John Johns, who ran the pub in 1914, appears to have been the last licensee.

The **Angel** just up the road is still open, despite the best efforts of the Dyffryn and Cleddau Temperance Union which in April 1925 objected to the renewal of the licence on the usual grounds of 'redundancy'. The temperance people thought there were too many pubs in Llandysilio (although one would probably have been too many for them). The Baptist minister from Blaenconyn chapel duly turned up in court bearing a petition signed by 130 local worthies calling for the inn to be closed. Fortunately, on this occasion the magistrates were on the side of the Angel and voted to keep the pub open. The licensee at the time was Mrs. Mary Jane Rees.

First mentioned in an 1844 newspaper report, the Angel was run by John Henton and his wife Elizabeth from 1851 to 1861. From 1867 to 1874 the Angel was kept by Ann Williams, while a widow named Anne Reynolds had charge in 1881. She was followed by her son-in-law Stephen Lewis in 1891,

A gathering outside the Angel in Llandysilio in the early 20th century.
Picture courtesy of Mr. Peter Phillips.

David Narbett in 1901 and Thomas Jenkins in 1906. William Rees was there in 1914 followed by various members of the Rees family, while Thomas Laugharne kept the pub from 1930 to 1946. There was a fairly regular turnover of licensees in the years after the Second World War, although Ernest Harper in the 1960s and Len Narbett in the 1970s provided some continuity. The present licensee is Anne Youngman who has been at the Angel since 1984.

A couple of other ale-houses are named as having existed in the village, although their exact location is hard to pin-point after nearly 150 years. Samuel Evans ran the **Duke of Wellington** throughout the 1850s, while there are several references to a pub variously called the **Sun** or the **Rising Sun**. Morgan Jones opened an ale-house called the Sun in 1827 and he was still there the

A recent photograph of the Angel.

following year, while Amy Jones ran the Sun in 1841 and Benjamin Lewis kept an ale-house called the Rising Sun according to a trade directory of 1867.

The **Bush** on the northern edge of the village was almost completely rebuilt in the 1990s. The original building was a typical farmhouse pub and Stephen Owens was licensee from 1822 to 1841. In 1848 the landlady was his widow, Mrs. Mary Owens, who also farmed the 82 acres that went with the pub. Evan Owens was the landlord from 1867 to 1871 and the landlady in 1874 was his wife — or possibly widow — Maria Owens.

Thomas Edwards, who was landlord in the 1890s, was the son of Rees Edwards of the Masons' Arms in Clunderwen. While running the Bush he was one of four men charged in connection with a *Ceffyl Pren* (wooden horse) incident which the press labelled 'The Clunderwen outrage'. During this incident, a woman from Clunderwen was dragged from her home at midnight by a jeering mob and paraded along the road between the two villages. Evidently she had been adjudged guilty of some moral misde-meanour and this was the rough and ready punishment traditionally meted out in rural Wales.

Quite probably Thomas Edwards and his companions were also involved in the 'tithe wars' of the 1890s when riots broke out in the countryside over the vexed issue of paying tithes to the Anglican church. Nonconformist farmers,

An early view of the Bush Inn, Llandysilio.
Picture courtesy of Mr. Roger Davies.

The Bush in the 1980s.
Picture courtesy of Mr. Peter Phillips.

who had no interest in the established church, were nevertheless expected to support it to the tune of one tenth of their earnings. In Llandysilio, where most people were chapel-goers and where memories of the Rebecca Riots were still fresh, there were many violent scenes as the authorities attempted to collect tithe arrears and fees. More than 20 policemen were drafted in when an auction of distrained cattle was held at a farm near Llandysilio in 1891; as they left the farm the auctioneer and the police were pelted with rotten eggs, turnips and turf

The rebuilt Bush as it looks today.

by an angry mob. No doubt this incident was recounted — and embellished — in the bar of the Bush Inn that evening.

James Davies was the landlord from 1901 to 1906, James Evans was there in 1914, while Mrs. Sophie Morgan was the landlady from 1923 to 1928. It was described as being 'badly conducted' in her day, and she was often fined for serving out of hours. The Bush was a regular haunt of passing Gypsies who would break their journey at the pub, and Mrs. Morgan would invariably draw a pint or two for them to drink with their bread and cheese, no matter what time of day it was — which is why she kept getting into trouble with the law.

Things didn't really improve after she left and there were half-a-dozen changes of licensee in the 1930s before Benjamin Harries took over and ran the pub throughout the 1940s, followed by Mr. and Mrs. Billy Harries who kept the Bush in the 1950s. David Gavin was the landlord throughout the 1960s followed by Ken and Josie Honeker. The Bush was almost completely rebuilt in the early 1990s by licensees Calum and Erika Wilson and they remained for a further ten years before handing over to present licensees John and Margaret Williams.

The landlord of the **New Inn** in 1867 was Daniel Owen who ran the pub until the 1880s when he was over 80; it seems to have expired when he did. The New Inn was a couple of miles north of Llandysilio, and seems to have been near the crossroads where roads lead to Rhydwilym and Rhydymoch — in which case it might not have been in Pembrokeshire at all.

CHAPTER FIFTEEN

Maenclochog, Rosebush, Penffordd and New Moat

Above the so-called 'Landsker line' the countryside is emptier than in the more fertile south — sparsely-populated farmland, watered by a network of streams which hurry southwards through wooded valleys from their source on the boggy Preseli moors. A few villages are dotted about, and each seems to have had its own small pub at one time or another.

The 'capital' of the area is Maenclochog, which has long been the main trading post for this scattered community of moorland farms, villages and slate quarries. As such it has always been generously supplied with pubs, as well as rural tradesmen of every description. The village's central position also meant that regular sheep and horse fairs were held there, attracting buyers and sellers from far and wide; as the historian Richard Fenton remarked in the early 19th century: 'There is a greater number of fairs there than in any other part of the county'.

Numerous illicit ale-houses opened on fair day, where home-brewed beer would be poured out of tea-pots into enamel mugs to hoodwink any watching policeman into thinking that nothing stronger than tea was being served. The following colourful description of Maenclochog fair in its hey-day, written by Mr. Tom Evans of Horeb, appears in *Llyfr Lloffion Maenclochog*, the village history compiled by Margaret (Peggy) Williams:

> Almost every house in the village at the time of the fair was an unlicensed tavern, brewing beer for sale cheaper than the inns. Tavern keepers from the surrounding district would come to sell beer in tents. Because there was so much beer there would be a lot of drunkenness with resultant fighting. Lads from one parish would oppose lads from another and fight with sticks and cudgels. Many would go home from the fair with injuries.

The village can claim a notable early drunkard. In 1743, the churchwardens were obliged to petition the Bishop of St. David's for the removal of

Cattle and horse traders gather on Maenclochog village green.

their vicar, William Crowther, on the grounds that 'he was seen so drunk in the parish church of Maenclochog last November that he could not marry a couple that attended there for that purpose'. There was one inn in the parish in 1782, run by John Perkins, while John Rogers was a publican in Maenclochog in 1795. Many more pubs opened in the area following the development of the slate quarries in the 19th century and the coming of the railway.

No doubt as a reaction to the large number of pubs in Maenclochog, a strong temperance movement grew up in the village. In 1898 it was stated that Maenclochog had a Rechabite preacher, a Rechabite schoolmaster and a Rechabite policeman, while a man named Alfred Howell did his best to counter the heavy drinking on fair day by opening a 'Blue Ribbon' tent which served (genuine) tea and buns.

Approaching from the south, the first of the Maenclochog pubs to be encountered would have been the **Kilmoor** just outside the village. David Gibby farmed here in the mid-19th century, and in the 1860s and '70s he ran an ale-house at the farm — no doubt benefiting in later years from the building of the Maenclochog railway which skirted his property.

At the entrance to the village was the **Step In** which was almost certainly a pub in its day — although when that day actually occurred is hard to say because it doesn't appear to have been licensed within the past couple of hundred years. A short distance to the west was a more recent hostelry, the **Railway Hotel**, which opened in September 1876 near Maenclochog station. A mason from Saundersfoot named Edwin Davies was landlord in 1881, David Evans was there in 1891 and insurance agent John Price Davies was the licensee in 1901. A part of the James Williams empire, the Railway was run by Daniel Howell from 1906 to 1914 and by Mrs. Adelaide James from

The Railway Hotel once served Maenclochog station.

1923 to 1947. She was followed by George Taliesin James and then Howell Haig James who was there in the 1950s. Miss Emmy Williams was the licensee from 1961 until the inn closed in the 1980s.

Most of Maenclochog's pubs were scattered around the large village green where the fairs and cattle markets were held. One of the earliest recorded pubs in the village was the **Serjeants Inn** which changed its name in 1818 to become the **Castle** — possibly inspired by Fenton's rather dubious assertion that the village was originally defended by a castle 'of whose siege and demolition in general terms we read in the Welsh Chronicles'. Simon Davies was the landlord between 1810 and 1841 when he was 60; during the early part of his tenure several stormy meetings were held at the inn regarding the enclosure of common land on the Preseli Hills. David Evans held the licence prior to his

The long-serving Joshua Thomas was the licensee of the Castle Inn. Maenclochog, when this picture was taken in about 1910.

Picture courtesy of Mr. Roger Davies.

179

death in 1846, after which the Castle seems to have been closed for a period before being rebuilt on a surprisingly ambitious scale. Stephen Howell was the licensee from 1864 to 1875 and the wonderfully-named Caleb Melchior was landlord in 1882, also farming about 30 acres. Heyday of the Castle Inn was during the days of long-serving licensee

The Castle as it looked in 2002.

Joshua William Thomas, a local farmer who ran the inn from 1891 to 1941. During his time a shop and pharmacy occupied part of the building and the Castle Inn became one of the area's main social and commercial centres. He was followed by Margaret Thomas and when she retired a few years later, Noel Prickard took over. George Roberts was in charge in the 1950s, followed by Will and Ruthie Jenkins, but this fine old pub closed about 16 years ago and is now looking sadly forlorn.

Another early pub fronting the green was the **Plough** where Alexander Thomas was the innkeeper from 1810 to 1813 and John Hugh was the landlord from 1822 to 1827. By 1841 the pub was being run by Martha Howell, while an elderly widower named David Howell ran the Plough from 1851 to 1861. The Plough was still going in 1867 when David Philip was the landlord, but the building — which stood alongside the Castle Inn — was unoccupied at the time of the 1871 census and appears never to have reopened.

The **Black Lion** stood close to the Vicarage and in 1841 it was being run by David Jones. Innkeeper, merchant and farmer Stephen Howell and his wife Harriet ran the Black Lion throughout the 1850s before moving to the Castle Inn, after which there are no further sightings of a pub of that name.

The closure of the Black Lion seems to have prompted local farmer Stephen Phillips to open the **Drovers' Arms** more or less next door; he was certainly running the pub from 1867 to 1875. It is believed that the Drovers' was located in the stone farmhouse tucked away behind Siop y Sgwar.

Just off the village green, on the Crymych road, was the **Swan**. David Phillips, quarryman and grocer, was in charge at the Swan for much of the 19th century, followed by his son, another David. For how much of that time the Swan also doubled as an ale-house is difficult to determine; possibly it

The former Drovers' Arms in Maenclochog.

The Swan once doubled as an inn and grocery shop.

only opened its doors on fair days. The Swan is now a private house called Arwel.

John Luke was farming at a village smallholding called Newgate at the time of the 1841 census, but ten years later he had opened the **Farmers' Arms** with his wife Elizabeth and they remained the licensees until 1867. William Evans was landlord in 1871, John Howell was there in 1875 and a carpenter from St. David's called Thomas Young ran the pub in 1881 with the help of his sister, Mary. The landlord and owner from 1895 onwards was a cooper named William Eynon and when he died in 1925 the licence passed to his daughter, Miss Mildred Eynon. She was still there in 1934 when the pub was forced to close under the redundancy ruling — the magistrates considering there were more than enough pubs in Maenclochog. Miss Eynon received a healthy £450 in compensation and the Farmers' later became the village police station before eventually being demolished and replaced by a bungalow.

Fortunately the **Globe** is still with us and this traditional village local is now the only pub in Maenclochog. The landlord from 1841 to 1871 was a quarryman named Robert Jones. Essex Rees from Treffgarne took over and was landlord between 1875 and 1882, purchasing the pub for £210 in June 1879 at the time of the break-up of the Maenclochog estate. John Llewellyn took charge of the Globe from 1891 to 1895 while Essex Rees continued to run an ironmongery business and the village post office from part of the premises. James James was the long-serving landlord from 1901 to 1945, by which time the pub had become a Buckley's house. A member of the

An early postcard view of the Globe Inn, Maenclochog.
Picture courtesy of Mr. Roger Davies.

The Globe was the last remaining Maenclochog pub when this photo was taken in 2003.

family which also ran the nearby Railway Hotel, Mr. James was succeeded by his widow, Mrs. Mary James, who bought the pub from Buckley's Brewery in 1952 and died two years later aged 88. The James' daughter, Mrs. Olwyn Percival, then took over and continued running the Globe until 1993, since when her son, Terry, has carried on the family tradition.

In the centre of the village, opposite the school, is Star Farm which seems to have been an ale-house for a time. Mary Evans, who lived there in the 1860s, is described as the innkeeper of the **Star** in a trade directory of 1867, and the Star Inn was mentioned in the *Welshman* of June 1879 in connection with an auction sale. Possibly, like the Swan, this was only an ale-house which came alive on fair days. The same probably applied to the **Union** where the landlord in 1867 was William Phillips who farmed at Penuchafydre at the top end of the village.

When slate quarrying began in the hills above Maenclochog isn't known, but the industry really took off in the 1820s thanks mainly to the efforts of landowner Joseph Foster Barham of Trecwn whose estates stretched across the Preselis. When his initial attempt to open up Craig-y-cwm quarry on the remote slopes of Foel Cwmcerwyn came to nothing, he switched his attention to the more accessible Bellstone quarry just north of Rosebush (Bellstone is an English translation of Maenclochog). By 1826, Barham was employing over 60 men at the quarry — slate-cutters, labourers and quarrymen.

Naturally enough, a number of ale-houses sprang up to cater for these well paid and hard-drinking slate-workers. The **General Picton** (run by James Phillips) and the **Lion** (Elizabeth Gibby) both appeared in 1823, while in 1826 no fewer than six ale-houses opened in Maenclochog parish as prospects looked bright for the Bellstone quarry. These were the **Black Horse,** which was opened by a farmer named Benjamin Howells; the **Coopers' Arms** opened by Thomas Thomas who was, unsurprisingly, a cooper by trade; the **Masons' Arms** run by stonemason Stephen Higgon; the **Square and Compass** which was run by Thomas David; the **Emborough Castle** run by James Phillips (presumably they meant 'Edinburgh' but that's the way it's pronounced in Pembrokeshire); and the **Union** where a farmer named Job Griffiths took out the licence. (Whether this Union was the same place as the one mentioned above is unclear).

With the possible exception of the Union, none of these ale-houses survived very long. As Alun John Richards explained in his book *The Slate Quarries of Pembrokeshire*, the workforce at the Bellstone quarry soon began to dwindle, and within a year Barham's payroll had fallen to just ten men. This was hardly enough to keep one publican in business, let alone six, so as quickly as they had opened, the quarrymen's ale-houses all closed. It is impossible now to know where they once stood, but since the quarries all lay to the north of Maenclochog village, probably the ale-houses did as well. It is interesting that in a strongly Welsh-speaking area, all the pubs had English signs — either an indication that the quarry workforce comprised English speakers or that the licensing authorities couldn't cope with Welsh names.

After the initial burst of slate quarrying at Rosebush in the 1820s, the industry stagnated for a number of years and only a handful of men were engaged in slate production. However the nationwide house-building boom of the 1860s vastly increased demand for roofing slate and slabs.

Considerable investment was made at Rosebush quarry which turned it into the most up-to-date and productive in Pembrokeshire, and at its peak it employed 100 men, many of whom lived in the row of cottages known as Rosebush Terrace.

To transport the slates away from Rosebush a railway was built in the 1870s linking the quarry with the main London line near Clunderwen. Unfortunately, no sooner was the railway finished than the bottom dropped out of the slate market and Rosebush found itself unable to compete with the huge north Wales quarries. In what appears to have been an act of despera-

The Prescelly Hotel was under threat of demolition when this photograph was taken in the early 1990s.

tion, a campaign was launched to promote Rosebush as a health resort, easily accessible by rail. The quarry-owners publicised the wild scenery and health-giving mountain air of the Preselis, and the area in front of the **Prescelly Hotel** was landscaped with ponds and fountains. However, despite a well-orchestrated publicity campaign, Rosebush never flourished as a health spa.

Other even more ambitious plans were carried forward, however, including extending the railway through Puncheston to Letterston and on to Goodwick where it was hoped that a ferry link to Ireland would be established. Work began in 1879, and on 1 November 1880, it was reported that:

> the Hon. Mrs. Owen of Rosebush gave an excellent dinner at the Prescelly Inn to the workmen of Messrs. Appleby and Lawton, contrac-
> tors of the Rosebush and Fishguard Railway, on the occasion of joining the two big banks on the above railway which completes the line to New Inn where the first station is to be.

The Prescelly Hotel was a prefabricated iron building, erected in 1876, and as with the Iron Duke at Clunderwen the sections would have arrived by train. A widow from Loughor named Anne Phillips kept the Prescelly Hotel in 1880, Mary and Gad Edwards were there from 1889 to 1891 and Thomas Harries was landlord in 1895. Charles Beckett ran the hotel from 1901 to 1906, Mrs. Elizabeth Jenkins was there from 1912 to 1923 and she was followed by Emily George. One of the best remembered of the Prescelly Hotel licensees was David Ernest Lewis who was in charge of the 'Tin Shed' throughout the 1930s, serving customers in the cosy, one-room bar with beer straight from the barrel. Mr. Lewis and his wife Louisa — a sister of Olwyn Percival of the Globe in Maenclochog — left to take over the licence of the Picton Inn at Clarbeston Road in 1940, subsequently moving to the Queen's Hotel in Haverfordwest.

Mr. Lewis' brother James Gomer 'Gom' Lewis and his wife Peg took over as licensees of the Prescelly Hotel and the remarkable Mrs. Lewis remained at the pub for over 50 years, working 12 hour days, seven days a week until she was well into her 70s. Following her death in the early 1990s the hotel closed and its days appeared to be numbered. Owners James Williams regarded the business as being 'not commercially viable', and instead of looking for new tenants the wine merchants put the property on the market in 1992. Estate agents King Thomas Lloyd Jones declared that the building was in such a poor state of repair that it would cost too much to renovate it and reopen it as a pub. 'We are looking at it as an ideal site for starter homes', said a spokesman.

Happily, both James Williams and the estate agents were proven wrong, because locals Brian and Brenda Llewellyn bought the unique building for £18,000, renovated it and reopened it as a traditional Welsh pub. Under the new

The restored Prescelly Hotel — now Tafarn Sinc.

185

name of **Tafarn Sinc,** and with a coat of red paint, it has since become one of Pembrokeshire's most popular and best-known country inns with lots of interesting artefacts recalling the history of the local slate and farming industries.

Nowadays a private house, the **New Inn** was once a crossroads inn and smallholding high in the Preselis — a halfway house on the mountain road from Haverfordwest to Cardigan where George Bowen was the landlord in 1784. J.T. Barber passed this way in 1803 as part of his *Tour Throughout South Wales.* 'In this dreary track stands a poor solitary house called New Inn', he wrote. 'However I here obtained part of a goose for my dinner'. He was followed in 1804 by another early travel writer, Benjamin Heath Malkin. 'A late traveller has informed the public that he got part of a goose for his dinner at the New Inn', grumbled Malkin. 'I much fear lest this anecdote should be the means of deluding future travellers with false hopes, for I could get nothing'.

Stephen Rowlands was the landlord from 1810 to 1828, while in February 1835 over 50 people gathered at the inn for a housewarming party to welcome new landlord Mr. Mark Bevan. According to the *Welshman* newspaper: 'The house has been lately rebuilt and from its situation and superior accommodations promises to promote the convenience of persons travelling between Haverfordwest and Cardigan'. Mr. Bevan rechristened the inn the **Nantyddwylan Arms**.

There is a story about this lonely inn and the quality of its beer in *The History of Haverfordwest and some Pembrokeshire Parishes.* In about the time that Mr. Bevan was running the pub, one of the learned judges who travelled the west Wales circuit was making his way on horseback over the arduous mountain trail when he decided to break the journey at the Nantyddwylan Arms.

> Here a flagon of beer was called for by his Lordship who, having tasted it with the air of a connoisseur, required the attendance of the landlord. Cap in hand mine host appeared. 'Pray, landlord', said his Lordship, 'tell me where you procure the malt with which you brewed this ale?' 'From Ha'rfordwest, my Lord'. 'Then, where do you get the water from?' 'From handy-by, my Lord', said the gratified landlord. 'Ah!' said his Lordship, 'it is just as I thought. If you had to go to Haverfordwest for the water, and had the malt been handy-by, the ale, I opine, would have been much better'.

Mark Bevan was succeeded in 1840 by John Furlong who assured sporting gentlemen of a comfortable residence during the shooting and hunting seasons. 'Excellent old wines, post chaises, neat cars, strong horses and careful drivers' were among the pub's attractions. Mr. Furlong certainly knew all about the local shooting preserves; in 1845 he was fined

The New Inn at Rosebush early in the last century.
Picture courtesy of Mr. Roger Davies.

20 shillings for poaching on the Barham estate at Henry's Moat. He left two years later to open the Great Western in Fishguard.

William and Martha Pritchard took over as innkeepers in 1849 and in 1855 Mr. Pritchard was fined £2 12s. for selling cigars without a licence to passengers aboard the rival *Cymro* and *Prince of Wales* coaches which called at the inn on their way between Cardigan and Haverfordwest. Following her husband's death, Martha Pritchard remained the licensee until well into the 1880s, by which time the pub had its own railway halt. Since 'Nantyddwylan Arms' was a bit of a mouthful, the halt was called 'New Inn' and the pub seems to have followed suit.

Farmer and publican David Edwards was the landlord by 1891 and the Edwards family continued to run the New Inn and farm the land for over 50 years. Until the 1930s they continued to brew their own beer in a 50-gallon copper boiler, selling the home-brew at sixpence a pint to the travellers, hill farmers, rabbit-catchers (and poachers) who made up

An advertisement for the New Inn in the 1950s.

187

The New Inn had closed when this photograph was taken in 2003.

the regular customers of this isolated inn. Excitement came with the visit of Wombwells travelling circus which broke its journey to Cardigan at the inn, with three elephants being housed overnight in the coachhouse! (Mr. Peter Denzil Edwards has written a marvellous account of *Fifty years and more at the New Inn* which is available at the County Library in Haverfordwest and makes fascinating reading).

Mrs. Gwenfra Dennis, a daughter of Tenby auctioneer Mr. F.B. Mason, leased the New Inn in the mid-1950s before going on to run the Bear at Crickhowell with great success for many years. The New Inn was then run by owners Mr. and Mrs. N.H. Woodhead who converted the coach house and stables next door to the pub into accommodation for parties of visiting anglers. The pub changed hands a couple of times after the Woodheads left, being bought in 1980 by an English couple, George and Peggy Edwards, who paid £68,000 for the business, only to discover that trade wasn't as brisk as they expected. In an effort to drum up custom they decided to introduce topless barmaids — a novelty anywhere in Pembrokeshire, let alone among the sheep farms of the Preselis. The move attracted both a great deal of publicity and also a fair amount of animosity, without really boosting trade.

Eventually, in desperation, George Edwards arranged for the New Inn to be burnt down while he and his wife were on holiday in Spain. Welsh language slogans daubed on the walls were meant to make the police think that Welsh extremists were responsible for the arson attack which gutted the old building, but it soon became obvious that Edwards was behind the blaze, his plan being to defraud his insurance company. Edwards eventually appeared at Carmarthen Crown Court on arson and conspiracy charges and was duly sent to prison.

Fortunately, the New Inn was rescued by former Fishguard antiques dealer Jane Wilson who bought the pub in 1984 and set about rebuilding and restoring it, keeping the outward appearance but modernising the interior. This gave the inn a new lease of life and for a while it was a popular out-of-town destination, being known for its good food and live music nights. However, its position in the middle of nowhere meant that the New Inn was always going to find it hard to survive and about three years ago it closed, apparently for good.

South of Maenclochog is nowadays something of a desert as far as pubs are concerned, but there was a time when there were a few inns dotted about the countryside. Anne Griffiths ran the **Cross Inn** in New Moat parish in the 1820s, although where this pub was is unknown. And a farmer's widow named Catherine Owen ran the **Ivy Bush** in New Moat village from 1851 to 1871. Her widowed daughter Mrs. Martha Davies was the only other land-lady, running the pub from 1875 to 1910, by which time she was nearly 80. A cottage pub, the Ivy Bush stood opposite Upper Moat Farm but has since been demolished.

Three generations of the same family ran the **Cross Inn** at Penffordd and farmed the smallholding that went with it. William Evans was the landlord from 1861 to 1881 and his daughter Martha married Philip Phillips who eventually became the licensee. In 1924 Philip Phillips died and the licence was transferred to his daughter Mary Phillips who subsequently ran the pub with her sister Elizabeth. But by then the Cross had been targeted by the Dyffryn and Cleddau Temperance Union which tried and failed in April 1925 to get the licence quashed on the usual grounds of 'redundancy'. However they had better luck in 1935 when the combined forces of the local temper-ance society, the vicar of Llawhaden and the Presbyterian minister of Penffordd persuaded the licensing justices that the inn — which had been empty for six months anyway — was surplus to requirements. The pub, which had once been a popular rendezvous for Gypsies and other travellers to the fairs at Maenclochog, was never opened again after February 1935 and it is now a cottage called Hafod Lon.

For some reason there were a couple of ale-houses on the country road between Penffordd and Bigny Cross. Anne James was licensee of the **Fox and Hounds** from the late 1820s until 1841, when she was 60. When this pub closed a couple of years later, Thomas Jones, tailor and innkeeper, opened the **Halfway House** nearby; he was still the licensee in 1851 but had settled for just being a tailor by 1861.

Between Bigny Cross and Llandysilio is a five-way crossroads known locally as Eden Cross. Farmer Griffith Thomas opened the **Cross Arms** on this junction in the late 1860s, no doubt with an eye on the railway line from Clunderwen to Rosebush which was planned to pass along the valley close to the pub. In due course the Cross Arms did indeed attract its share of hard-drinking navvies employed to build the line. These workmen came from England, Ireland and Wales, and the animosity which existed between the various nationalities erupted in October 1874 when an English navvy was attacked and beaten so badly that he later died of his injuries. The inquest was held at the Cross Arms when a verdict of murder was returned. Brothers Joseph and Nathaniel Evans and a third man named John Williams later stood trial for the murder, but all three were acquitted by a jury in Haverfordwest — to the astonishment of most people in the courtroom.

Griffith Thomas and his wife Margaret continued to run the Cross Arms into the 1880s, while Margaret was there on her own in the 1890s. Morris James kept the pub in 1906, Mrs. Mary James held the licence in 1914 and William Jacob was there in 1923. Although the official name of the pub was Cross Arms, locals always called it 'Eden' after the crossroads. In 1927 the licence passed to Thomas Laugharne, but the licence wasn't renewed in 1929 and Mr. Laugharne departed from 'Eden' to Llandysilio where he continued the biblical theme by taking charge of the Angel.

Bibliography

Much of the information in this book has been gleaned from old newspapers, notably the *Welshman*, the *Carmarthen Journal*, the *Tenby Observer*, the *Pembrokeshire Herald*, the *Narberth Weekly Observer* and the *West Wales Guardian*.

The various trade directories have also proved very useful, particularly those published at various times between 1811 and 1925 by Slater, Kelly, Pigot, Holden and Hunt.

General

Ale and Hearty. Alan Wykes, 1979.
Drink and the Victorians. Brian Harrison, 1971.
Farmhouse Brewing. Elfyn Scourfield, 1974.
British Brewing. Gavin Smith, 2004.
The English Pub. Peter Haydon, 1994.
The English Pub. Michael Jackson, 1976.
The Old Inns of England. A.E. Richardson, 1934.
Prince of Ales - The History of Brewing in Wales. Brian Glover, 1993.
The Pubs of Leominster, Kington and North-west Herefordshire. Ron Shoesmith
    and Roger Barrett, 2000.
Victuallers' Licences. Jeremy Gibson and Judith Hunter, 1997.
Welsh Pub Names. Myrddin ap Dafydd, 1991.
The Wordsworth Dictionary of Pub Names. Leslie Dunkling and Gordon
    Wright, 1994.
*Wales' Maritime Trade in Wine During the Later Middle Ages (Maritime
Wales, 1992).* K. Lloyd Gruffydd.
The Welsh Sunday Closing Act 1881 (Article in *The Welsh History Review*,
    December 1972). W.R. Lambert

Pembrokeshire

The Antiquities of Laugharne. Mary Curtis, 1880.
From Amroth to Utah. Roscoe Howells, 2001.
Amroth — A Brief History. Roscoe Howells, 2000.
Baptist Historical Sketches of Pembrokeshire. Rev. R.C. Roberts, 1907.
Best Pub Walks in Pembrokeshire. Laurence Main, 1994.

A Calendar of the Public Records relating to Pembrokeshire.
Cymmrodorion Record Series, 1911.
The Cambrian Directory. 1800.
Cambrian Tourist. G.R. Whittaker, 1821 (fifth edition).
Descriptive Excursions Through South Wales and Monmouthshire.
        E. Donovan, 1804.
The Description of Pembrokshire. George Owen, 1603; ed. Henry Owen 1906.
Donovan's South Wales. E. Donovan, 1805.
Flow Gently Sweet River. Dr. Robert Davies, 2003.
A Guide to Pembrokeshire Inns and Pubs. Michael Fitzgerald.
A History of Ludchurch. A. Eric Evans, 1994.
A Historical Tour Through Pembrokeshire. Richard Fenton, 1811.
The History of Little England Beyond Wales. Edward Laws, 1888.
History of Haverfordwest and some Pembrokeshire Parishes. John Brown.
The Inn Crowd (1st and 2nd editions). C.I. Thomas (publ.).
Industrial Saundersfoot. M.R.C. Price, 1982.
Llanteg Down the Years (vols 1 - 3). Llanteg Local History Society.
The 'Landsker Borderlands' series of publications, SPARC (publ.).
Llyfr Lloffion Maenclochog. Compiled by Margaret (Peggy) Williams.
Memoranda of the Late Col. John Owen of Rosebush. 1893.
Narberth — Images of the Past. Pauline Griffiths and Ann Keen.
Nicholson's Cambrian Travellers' Guide. 1840.
Pembroke People. Richard Rose, 2000.
Pembrokeshire County History, Vol III. Brian Howells (ed.).
Pembrokeshire - The Forgotten Coalfield. M.R. Connop-Price, 2004.
Pembrokeshire in By-gone Days (West Wales Historical Records. Vol IX).
        Francis Green.
Pembrokeshire Life: 1572-1843. B. and K. Howells (eds).
A Pembrokeshire Countryman Looks Back. W.R. Morgan, 1988.
The Place-names of Pembrokeshire. B.G. Charles, 1992.
The Oxford, Gloucester and Milford Haven Road. Charles Harper, 1905.
Romilly's Visits to Wales. Edited by M.G.R. Morris, 1998.
The Railways of Pembrokeshire. John Morris, 1981.
A River Never Sleeps. Dr. Robert Davies, 2000.
The Slate Quarries of Pembrokeshire. Alun John Richards, 1998.
The Story of Narberth. Edited by M.G.R.Morris,1990.
The Story of Saundersfoot. T.G. Stickings, 1970.
The Story of Begelly. W.R. Morgan, 1980.
Tour Through a Part of South Wales. William Matthews, 1786.
*Tavernspite: A Meeting of the Ways (Journal of the Pembrokeshire
        Historical Society, No. 5).* M.G.R. Morris, 1992.
The Tithe War in Pembrokeshire. Pamela Horn, 1982.
Wanderings and Excursions in South Wales. Thomas Roscoe, 1821.
Historical Sketches of Pembroke Dock. George Mason, 1906.
Tour through South Wales. J.T. Barber, 1803.

Index

In the following index all pub names, old and new, are included — where there has been name changes they are cross-referenced and shown in brackets. 'Inn' is not normally used in the title (apart from 'New Inn'). To avoid confusion the parish or village is shown for country inns; In Narberth and Saundersfoot the street name is included. Page numbers in bold type indicate the main entry for that inn.

197